Off Watch

Off Watch
A Selection of Bunkside Reading

Edited by J J Skellorn

ADLARD COLES LIMITED
GRANADA PUBLISHING
London Toronto Sydney New York

Published by Granada Publishing in
Adlard Coles Limited, 1979

Granada Publishing Limited
Frogmore, St Albans, Herts AL2 2NF
and
3 Upper James Street, London WIR 4BP
Suite 405, 4th Floor, United Nations Plaza, New York, NY 10017, USA
Q164 Queen Victoria Buildings, Sydney, NSW 2000, Australia
100 Skyway Avenue, Toronto, Ontario, Canada M9W 3A6
PO Box 84165, Greenside, 2034 Johannesburg, South Africa
CML Centre, Queen and Wyndham, Auckland 1, New Zealand

ISBN 0 229 11610 8

Printed in Great Britain by
Fletcher & Son Ltd, Norwich

Contents

Editor's Introduction

Devotees of jogging can take a quick trip around the block whenever it suits them; golfers can practise putting on the living room or office floor; most other sportsmen can enjoy their hobby vicariously from the TV screen. But the lover of sailing needs water in large quantities before he can get the adrenalin working when not actually under way.

So this book is designed to help fill the gaps when the sailing man or woman is miles from the sea, or stormbound in port, or it's winter and too damn cold. Pick it up, dip into it, doze over it, but above all, sample the delights of some of the best maritime writing ever to appear in print. For here are some of the choicest nuggets of sailing wisdom ever collected together.

Adlard Coles Ltd have been publishing books on sailing for over forty years. The idea behind this book was that some of our authors should select their own favourite passages from their books, and tell us the reasons for their choice. We felt that we had to add some selections from the Mariner's Library, published by our sister list, Rupert Hart-Davis; similarly one or two other classics were too good to omit. But omissions there had to be, so if your favourite author is not represented, perhaps a future volume will remedy the defect.

Because we felt that the book should offer five minutes as well as fifty-five minutes of complete distraction, we have added some lighthearted magazine spoofs which have struck us as worthy of more permanent record. We have also illustrated it with some spectacular photographs, illustrating variously some comic, disastrous and awesome aspects of the sea and sailing.

We would like to thank all the authors, who entered into the spirit of the book, made selections and wrote introductions, and the photographers who racked their memories for the background to their unique photographs. I am especially grateful to Mr Adlard Coles for kindly agreeing to write the Foreword, in which he recounts the early history and development of the list.

We are grateful to the Arthur Ransome Estate for permission to reprint the extract from *Racundra's First Cruise*, originally published by Jonathan Cape Ltd, to the Alain Gerbault Estate and Anthony Shiel Associates Ltd for permission to reprint the extracts from *The Fight of the 'Firecrest'* and to Eric Newby for permission to reprint the extract from *The Last Grain Race*, originally published by Martin Secker and Warburg Ltd.

JJS
1979

Foreword

I hope the following notes about the early history of Adlard Coles Ltd may be of interest.

In 1933 I registered a small family company under the name of Robert Ross & Co Ltd in order to market some children's board games which I had invented; the name was an amalgamation of the christian name of my father-in-law, and the maiden name of my grandmother (after whom our son Ross had been called). Somewhat surprisingly, therefore, the first publications of the company were not books but nautical games. Among these were two I had invented as a schoolboy and which gave my wife and myself much pleasure when we played them with our children, and later with our grandchildren.

About this time we met a Mr Edmund Vale, an author of books on the sea and topography, who was a genius in his ideas, and he contributed some of his own inventions to the list, which sold well in their somewhat specialist market. Unfortunately, on the advice of the trade, the scope was widened to include cheaper products and the business got out of hand. The company began to make losses and the time arrived when it became necessary to cease further games production.

Happily, we had also published a few books, which helped to tide us over, but it was not until the end of World War II that I decided to take up publishing seriously as a profession. At this time, most of the leading general publishers were willing to consider an occasional yachting book, but the only two I remember to have had general yachting lists, including narratives, were Edward Arnold, a first-rate company with perhaps a dozen or more titles, including my own *Creeks and Harbours of the Solent* (which was first published in 1933), and Peter Davies who published the Uffa Fox books and a number of others. The first book we published immediately after the war was my *Sailing Days,* which was a happy book, I think, and quite a success. This was followed by Ian Proctor's *Racing Dinghy Handling* and his two other classics on the same subject. But what finally set the company on its feet was Captain John Illingworth's masterly work *Offshore.* I had been lucky enough to win the RORC Class III La Rochelle race, where, at the end of the race, the book was planned at a party in the Town Hall. It was first published in 1949 at £2.25 and I note with pleasure it is still in the list, together with the following which have all been into new editions (some of them many times) and have reprinted for over twenty-five years: *Sea Signalling Simplified* by Captain Russell (27p in 1949), *Yacht Construction* by C J Watts and later revised by Kenneth Jurd (£1.05 in 1950), *Sailing Yacht Design* by my old friend the late Douglas Phillips-Birt (£1.25 in 1952) and *Knots and Splices* by Cyrus Day (30p in 1953); in 1952 we also published Col 'Blondie' Hasler's *Harbours and Anchorages of the North Coast of Brittany,* which I later took on myself as *North Brittany Harbours.*

Setting up publishing after the war was tough for the 'new boys' such as myself, and we were all in open competition with the leading long-established publishers who had big back lists of successful books and, consequently, much lower overhead expenses at a time when price counted much more than it does today. I am afraid there were many casualties among the new publishers, but Robert Ross Ltd prospered in a modest way by deliberately keeping it small. I had the advantage of a specialised list and of being fairly well known, having started long-distance cruising as far back as 1923; I had also done a great deal of racing, besides already having eight yachting books to my credit, or discredit. Because of this, some in the book trade suggested that it might be better for the business to bear my own name so, after some deliberation, the name of the company was changed from Robert Ross to Adlard Coles Ltd in 1953. We had the privilege of first refusal of a considerable proportion of the new yachting books, including narratives of the long-distance voyages of the time. In addition we had a growing list of books on ships and shipping.

To cut a long story short, in the early 1960s we went into association with Rupert Hart-Davis Ltd, who had already published the legendary Mariner's Library, and became their subsidiary. Both companies were bought by Granada Publishing in December 1963 and I stayed on as Chairman of Adlard Coles Ltd until September 1967 before finally leaving by mutual agreement. One of the last books I commissioned was *Sails,* written by Jeremy Howard-Williams, the present Managing Editor.

I would like to end by congratulating all concerned with the current notable list of books, and add my best wishes for the success of this volume.

Lymington   K Adlard Coles
1979

The Way of a Ship in the Sea

The Way of a Ship in the Sea

Rosemary and Colin Mudie
Power Yachts
first published 1977

This extract is taken from the first chapter, which describes how a boat, especially a power craft, learns to live with the sea. The authors write:

'*We have a slight feeling that our publishers think that one of the most interesting facts about the background to* Power Yachts *is that it took ten years from contract to publication. This was, we hasten to say, not entirely due to procrastination on our part. The trouble was that as designers rather than authors we kept on being offered the most fascinating boats to design and had to beg extension after extension, sometimes officially and sometimes unofficially, in the delivery of the manuscript. An 80-foot yacht takes us between six months and a year to design and so the extensions we asked for were rarely small ones.*

'*Then again there is joint authorship. At first we were certain that this meant halving the work. This proved entirely wrong, not because we were disputatious about the content – far from it – but, by the time we had both assembled our lists of what it was essential to cover, we found ourselves contemplating a much larger volume than either of us had thought of in the contract stages. Then again, joint authorship involves a great deal of discussion and, while this is extremely valuable and a great pleasure in itself, it does tend to prolong the production of those neatly typed pages required by a patient publisher.*

'*We have always held strong views on power yachts. They have often tended to be considered as second-class citizens compared with sailing boats, and while this may have been true in the last century, it is certainly not so now. Sailing boats are lovely in themselves and only the most dismal versions are regarded as failures, but a power yacht is now often as complex as an aircraft and can be a disappointment if she is less than first class in every department. We wanted to try to put the principles of excellence in power yachts into our book, rather than to give a list of useful data or pages of design drawings which inevitably get out of date in a few years in this fast developing area of naval architecture.*

'*With regard to the actual format of the book, we did eventually think that the first chapter "The Way of a Ship in the Sea" plunged rather rapidly into some of the more complicated areas of seagoing and would have liked to put it later in the book. However, the suggestion of further holding up the production so shocked the editor that we dropped the idea like a hot potato.*'

Two thousand years ago (was it in the middle of the Sinai desert?) some sage declared that one of the biggest mysteries in the world was the way of a ship in the sea. Two thousand years more of daily use of oceans and a modicum of scientific research have passed and still there are many of us who cling to the same views. We look at ships and are eager to see mysteries instead of the often commonplace explanations. There are many, many mysteries left at a somewhat esoteric level, but by and large the greater part of the understanding of the way of a ship in the sea comes from looking for simple and logical explanations. We are perhaps still unable to translate our knowledge into the hard and rigid language of science, but this is more of a problem for interpreters than for practitioners.

Consider first then our ship, motor boat or motor yacht, sitting quietly at rest in flat water in complete equilibrium with the watery world all around. Then we start the engines and let in our ahead clutches to apply the propulsive power. Three things happen – at least three, that is, for the unexpected is always with us. However, the three main effects of applying the power are:

1. The thrust from the propulsive unit produces a couple about the centre of buoyancy of the boat. This can only be balanced by a change of hull trim. With a normal inboard engine arrangement the propeller thrust acts along the shaft line producing a couple to push the bows down, and the normal outboard engine would produce the opposite effect to push the bows up.

2. The forward thrust pushes the hull through the water.

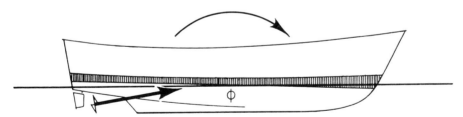

Fig. 1 The thrust of a well angled propeller shaft will push the bows down.

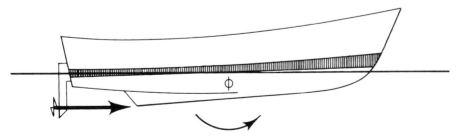

Fig. 2 The thrust from an outboard unit will push the bows up.

3. The water pushed aside by the bows sets up a wave system along the length of the hull. The arrangement of crests and hollows can also affect the basic buoyant trim of the hull. Some unbalanced power-thrust systems, such as a single propeller, can also affect athwartships trim from the simple effect of the torque.

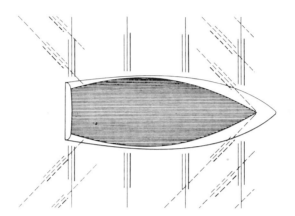

Fig. 3 The basic wave system set up around the hull.

The wave system divides itself into two distinct forms. From the bow and stern spring divergent waves running away diagonally from the craft and along the length of the hull; this develops a neat system of so-called transverse waves which travel at right angles to the hull and, of course, at the same speed. These transverse waves are a major factor in the performance of the craft in that the energy absorbed in creating them is the biggest factor in wave-making resistance at speed, and the attitude in which they leave the craft sitting is critical in considering the extra power required to drive her faster. The length between crests of a symmetrical standard wave form of the type set up around a craft is $\left(\dfrac{V}{1\cdot34}\right)^{2}$ and it is no coincidence that this can be rearranged, for waves, to take the form $\dfrac{V}{\sqrt{L}} = 1\cdot34$ and that the normal maximum speed for a boat is the same formula.

The ship moves forward accompanied by its train of waves, and the distance between the wave crests is proportional to the speed of the boat. It is also proportional to the square root of the waterline length of the craft, which therefore allows all craft to be compared on a relative speed basis. If V, the speed, divided by $\sqrt{L}$, the waterline length, is the same for two craft of different dimensions, they are operating the same kind of wave-making systems and are therefore open to comparison.

Fig. 4 The transverse wave system at $\frac{V}{\sqrt{L}}$ of about 0·75, say about 4½ knots for 36 ft waterline craft.

When V is measured in knots and L in feet it so happens that when $\frac{V}{\sqrt{L}}$ is unity the wave system has come down to two crests separated, of course, by a hollow. Up to this speed the craft is quite easily driven and is supported in a reasonably even manner by a number of wave crests which are comparatively small. At $\frac{V}{\sqrt{L}}$ of 1 the hull is nicely supported by a wave at each end. This also fits very happily the most convenient shape for making boats and some are especially designed round the wave form. This is the most efficient and economical speed at which to drive a boat.

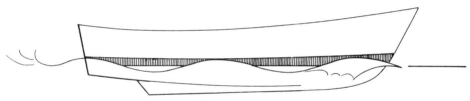

Fig. 5 The transverse wave system at $\frac{V}{\sqrt{L}}$ of about 0·9, say about 5½ knots for 36 ft waterline craft.

Above $\frac{V}{\sqrt{L}}$ of 1 the wave system starts to get longer than the boat and the support for the bow moves aft and the support for the stern also moves aft, tending to drop the aft end into the trough. The maximum practical speed at which the wave system still gives enough support for the vessel to travel in a reasonably respectable posture is somewhere between a $\frac{V}{\sqrt{L}}$ of

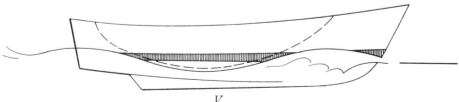

Fig. 6 The transverse wave system at $\frac{V}{\sqrt{L}}$ of about 1·2, say about 7¼ knots for 36 ft waterline craft. Note how the buttock line (shown by dotted line) can be designed to follow the wave form.

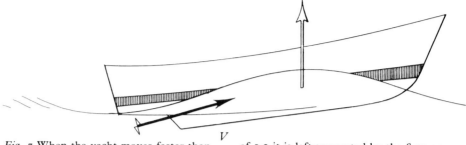

Fig. 7 When the yacht moves faster than $\dfrac{V}{\sqrt{L}}$ of 1·3 it is left supported by the first wave.

1·3 to 1·5̄, depending upon the hull form. Obviously the capacity of the shape of the vessel to make use of the stern wave makes a difference to the effective *L* which might be used instead of the nominal length measured by a ruler off the profile.

It is possible to use the coefficient of water-plane area, which indirectly indicates the fullness of the ends, as a factor to convert *L* to a more accurate figure for estimating the wave system, but once the principle is understood it is really not worth the trouble.

When the boat is powered to go faster than this the stern wave falls right aft of the stern and the hull is left climbing the bow wave. Quite a proportion of the combination of the buoyant lift from the bow wave and the thrust up the propeller shaft is directed now to push the hull upwards bodily. The buoyant lift is not a single force as shown in Fig. 7 but is spread all over the hull bottom and is approximately proportional to the depth below the surface. The water flow is, apart from the lift of the waves, practically horizontal and can be considered the equivalent of the boat standing still in moving water. This of course acts on all surfaces presented to it. On a surface inclined upwards, such as the bow lines of a boat, the resultant force is lift. On a surface inclined downwards, like the stern shapes of some sailing craft, the resultant force is downwards. The whole system has, as the usual natural law, to achieve an equilibrium and the situation looks like the example illustrated in Fig. 9.

With further speed the situation just gets worse and worse. The bow lifts and the stern drops until, sometimes, the craft is overwhelmed by sea pouring in over the stern. Very occasionally cavitation might set in but

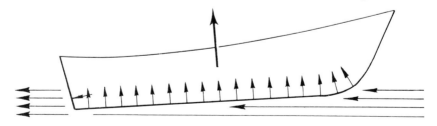

Fig. 8 If the hull surfaces are inclined to the water flow the hull will lift badly.

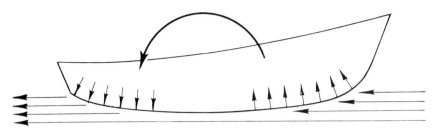

Fig. 9 If a substantial area is inclined away from the water flow then that end of the hull will sink until equilibrium is reached.

this, although reducing the suction aft, can create an even worse hazard with violent and irregular motions. These effects are commonly seen when children pull their toy boats too fast on their strings, and are very commonly heard about when small craft are towed towards safety by ships. The towing ship travels at its very modest $\dfrac{V}{\sqrt{L}}$ but this often represents a $\dfrac{V}{\sqrt{L}}$ well above that which is safe for the towed boat, which is then over-whelmed if it is not pulled to pieces. A 200-foot ship travelling at 15 knots has a $\dfrac{V}{\sqrt{L}}$ of just about 1, but the 20-foot boat it might tow would have to travel at a $\dfrac{V}{\sqrt{L}}$ of nearly 3·5 to stay with her. Fig. 7, however, just swallows its bow wave – really gets the buoyant lift right under the hull and aft of its centre of gravity (c.g.) so that the bow will drop and the craft remain supported both by the buoyancy of its hull and the pressure of the water.

Two possibilities can at once be seen: (1) the variation of lift possible by altering the angle at which the bottom is attacking the water; (2) the relief of drag by inducing a measure of cavitation or other form of breakaway in those parts where suction develops.

The simple wave system is, of course, above the slowest speeds often obscured by the spray flung off the top of the bow wave. Aft, the resurgent water appearing from under the boat and the jet thrust from the propellers also combine to obscure the system about and aft of the stern.

As the speed of the craft is increased even further the water pressures on the bottom increase and the proportional effect of the buoyancy reduces. The craft rises from the sea until it is virtually completely supported by the water pressure due to its speed, exactly as is a water skier who uses his personal buoyancy for support only in emergencies.

At slow speeds the craft is supported by its personal buoyancy and as this is equal to its displacement the slow speed hull is known as a displacement craft. At high speed the craft is supported principally from the action of planing across the top of the sea and this is therefore called a planing craft. Where the division comes is very hard to define exactly and there are increasing numbers of intermediate speed craft labelled semi-planing and semi-displacement craft. Many authorities give a speed of $\dfrac{V}{\sqrt{L}}$ of 3·5 as the bottom limit of true planing craft.

Heaving, Pitching and Rolling

Of all the terms in naval architecture which should be kept from the eyes and thoughts of a prospective owner, heave, pitch and roll must head the list. They are cold damp words to strike a chill in any heart warmed with thoughts of Riviera sunshine and not ready at great expense to be serious about the grey North Sea. However, as all boats nowadays are expected to be strong and safe, heaving, pitching and rolling cover a great part of what is thought to be seaworthiness.

Heaving is defined conveniently enough in the *Oxford Dictionary* as the 'force exerted by the swell of the sea on the course of a ship'. There is also another definition, but we will leave that out.

Since the swell of the sea is proportionally larger for the smaller craft, the effect of heave is probably more pronounced among yachts than ships. A swell of the sea under your counter at the wrong moment is one of the main factors in broaching-to, and a swell of the sea just to weather of your

Fig. 10 Heave is the movement of the craft by the sea itself.

bows can stop the swing of an underpowered craft through the wind. A convenient swell of the sea about amidships or aft has got many a reluctant overweight planing boat out of the sea to do its stuff. The heave is due entirely to the motion of the sea and is therefore only very broadly predictable. Wave heights and lengths and periods are theoretically averageable for different parts of the sea, but for a small craft it is often the waves inside the big waves which are important and these are rarely classified. The principal effect of heave, apart from inconveniencing the manoeuvres of the vessel, is to modify the natural pitching and rolling of the vessel. Pitch and roll are individual to each craft, and if a boat is set rolling or/and pitching in flat water it continues at the same rate damped only by the skin friction of the hull. In rough water it is modified, at any moment aided or opposed by the swell of the sea. The overall effect is further modified by the vessel's own wave train due to her own speed of advance through the seas, which can itself change from moment to moment in a seaway. This builds up a quite complicated system of factors to affect what a yacht hull is doing at any moment in the sea. The system is probably too complicated for any reasonable analysis except perhaps one day with a well briefed computer. However, the problem for the designer is much simplified. Only two criteria really need to be examined. First, is the motion acceptable to the humans on board? It is still fortunately the prime duty of a yacht to carry people and give them confident pleasure. This is approached principally through similarity with previous craft checked through reasonably simple calculations. The second criterion is that the natural period of the yacht in pitching and rolling should not be such as to cause a harmonic

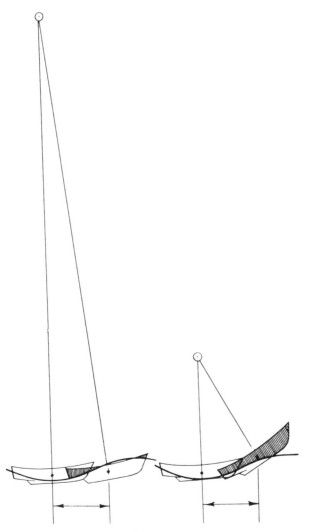

Fig. 11 The effect of the fore and aft pitching period in a seaway.

build-up of motion between the natural period of the yacht and the seas she is expected to encounter.

A yacht with a large fore and aft period (equivalent to a long pendulum motion) responds only slowly to a wave and therefore tends to plough straight into and through every sea in her path. This of course increases the hull resistance by including the full depth of the topsides in the bulk to be pushed along, thereby slowing the craft as well as making her unduly wet. However, if the yacht has a very short period, such as with all weight ridiculously concentrated amidships, she will lift quickly to the sea but will get in some more pitching off her own characteristics before she meets the next sea. We all know of boats like this of which it is remarked that they go up and down twice in the same hole.

The ideal is to produce a weight distribution fore and aft such that the hull lifts quickly and easily to the wave it encounters, and either damps out the motion quickly before the next wave comes along or is just lifting again

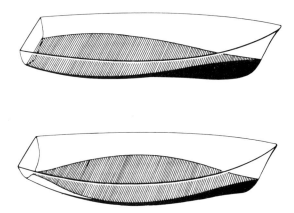

Fig. 12 The asymmetrical waterplane area will dampen periodic pitching in a light craft.

when it does. The former is probably the best characteristic to aim for in a design and leads into the question of damping out a fore and aft periodic motion. Natural skin friction is doing this all the time, but a quite heavy damping occurs if the fore and aft bodies are far from being symmetrical due to the effect of alternately immersing one end and the other as the yacht pitches.

Two generalisations can thus be offered. The first is that light craft with weights concentrated near amidships should perhaps be of fairly asymmetrical form fore and aft, and that heavy craft and those with weights well spread fore and aft should be more symmetrical fore and aft. This must be heavily qualified by adding that other features might considerably modify these requirements in a satisfactory yacht. Fortunately we have generations of experience of what is and what is not a good sea boat for most waters and therefore plenty of precedent, the designer's best friend, to call upon. Few yachts have their fore and aft metacentric height calculated, perhaps too few. It is a laborious calculation which doubtless will become routine computer work.

The athwartships calculations are much more commonly embarked upon because the roll of a yacht is rather more noticeable than its pitching, more alarming at times, and is part of the question of stability and therefore of basic safety. The period of encounter from the seas is slower when encountered beam-on compared with bow-on, and the yacht is very much smaller across its beam than fore and aft. The natural symmetry between the two sides also reduces the damping of the roll. Thus the natural period of roll has a much bigger chance to develop athwartships. A vessel of great stability that rolls quickly and sharply is probably very safe but often feels unsafe, whereas a vessel of modest stability that rolls wide and slowly often appears to respond and work with the sea in a confident manner. Here the designer has to know the type of motion which the owner or owners will feel happiest with (for tastes differ very widely in this respect) and ally it with a suitable stability and rolling period. Many an uncomfortable craft has been made more seaworthy by such apparent madnesses as hoisting anchors to the masthead or pumping out the ballast or freshwater tanks.

The effect of wind on a vessel is nearly always to steady it and to damp rolling. Sometimes small vessels are to be seen sporting large funnels and these are little more than aluminium steadying sails. The real thing of canvas, sticks and string is of course quite common on slower craft designed for open water use. All make use of the principle that energy is required, even on a windless day, to wave a large flat area through the air, and this energy can only come from that available to start the yacht rolling in the first place.

The natural skin friction of the hull has the same effect and this is often augmented by underwater fins and bilge keels. If the yacht is rolling *in* the sea with the motion stemming principally from its periodic characteristics, then skin friction and keels will reduce the roll. However, if the yacht is merely rolling *with* the sea, then the skin and keels will not be travelling across the waterflow and the motion will not be affected.

Roll damping fins are now quite common. These are little controllable underwater wings on each side of the yacht which can be quickly angled to give lift or downthrust. They are controlled directly from the angle of heel and are set to work with quite astonishing effect in direct opposition to the rolling. Their only real defect is that they rely on the forward speed of the craft for effect, while most marine emergencies cause a vessel to be slowed or even stopped at the time when freedom from rolling would be best appreciated.

Roll damping tank systems give their benefits whether the vessel is under way or not, but they are, at this time, very tricky in their operation.

In essence these systems consist of a half-filled tank fitted right outboard on each side of the craft. The tanks are connected by a pipe and the water is allowed to swill from tank to tank as the vessel rolls. The trick is so to control the water flow by means of the skin friction of the connecting pipe and a control valve as to get the through flow out of phase with the natural roll. The effect is rather as if the whole crew rushed to whichever rail was rising as the yacht rolled.

Another simple arrangement to reduce rolling in open waters has been called the 'Flopper Stopper'. This requires two large poles to be rigged either side of the yacht rather in the manner of fishermen's trolling rods; miniature paravanes are suspended from these into the sea. These are designed to drop easily through the water when their pole drops as the yacht rolls but to require some force to pull up again. By using long poles the leverage effect can be great and the actual size of the paravanes very small, so that their effect on the speed of the parent craft is small.

Yawing and Broaching

A combination of rolling, pitching and heaving and the effect of the hull characteristics can and do combine to make a craft depart from her proper course. In itself such yawing is of little account and, if steering is your pleasure, gives interest and the exercise of skill to enjoy during a passage. Yawing is usually at its most pronounced with a quartering sea, and when the seas become large the innocuous yaw can develop into the relatively

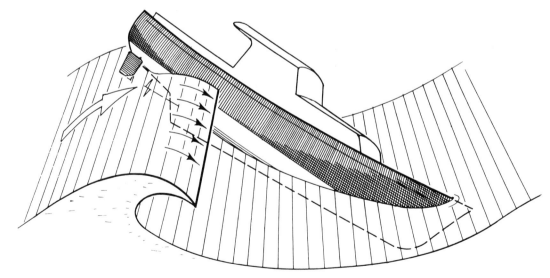

Fig. 13 The mechanics of broaching: the bow is braked strongly by immersion and the stern is carried forward both by the propellers and by the following wave crest. At the same time control is reduced by the rudders lifting out of solid water.

dangerous broach. Here the swing becomes uncontrollable and the vessel swings broadside-on to the seas in a trough. The accompanying roll leaves her at her most vulnerable to an initial capsize or to being inundated by the next crest.

In a light craft broaching is rarely more than a momentary annoyance in that the forces involved are small and the craft is more flung with the seas and tossed ahead by the following wave crest. In a bigger and heavier craft less able to respond the effect can be catastrophic. Broaching is therefore one of the greatest hazards to the motor yacht and its prevention requires consideration in the design as well as care by the seaman.

The basic mechanics of broaching are relatively simple. The yacht's bow rises over the wave crest and drops into the trough. The yacht runs down the front of the wave and buries the bow in the back of the next wave. The bow is held but the stern is still carried by the preceding wave and propelled by the engines. Unless careful control can be maintained over the direction of the craft the stern will swing to one side or other down the slope, until she finishes with some force broadside-on in the trough.

The two most obvious methods of reducing the broaching hazard are:

1. To shape the bow so that it digs in as little as possible and the stern so that it has as little buoyancy as possible to be caught and lifted. This would be allied with a distribution of weights so that the bow would be able to respond quickly as it hit the sea.
2. To shape the hull so that she tends to steer straight.

There is a limit to how far one can pursue the first possibility for we would like a fat scow-like bow and fine stern for anti-broaching, and the same shape the other way round for performance and going into the wind and sea. The second possibility is less obvious in a motor yacht except in terms of adding skegs and lateral area which, although excellent in reducing the possibility of a broach, can increase its violence when it does occur. However, a yaw really becomes uncontrollable once the vessel takes up an angle of heel, when two things happen. The natural shape of the hull, fair and symmetrical when upright, becomes often quite banana-shaped with a strong, often uncontrollable, built-in self-steering effect. The yacht also rises bodily when heeled, often raising one if not both rudders into the surface spindrift where they have virtually no effect.

The best self-steering hull forms have long straight buttock lines aft and the problem then becomes one of allying these with a bow form of matching fullness and at the same time getting the rudder or rudders nice and deep without too much keel or skeg right aft.

Broaching is also affected by the speed at which the yacht is running in the sea, for the faster she is travelling the further she is likely to plunge her bow into the sea ahead and fling her stern after it. In a high-powered vessel the steering value of the engines in these conditions can be considerable, and if the engine throttle or speed controls are easily and readily to hand many an incipient broach can be stopped by a burst of speed or by pulling back one of a pair of engines. Eventually, however, the vessel will become virtually wind propelled in the worst conditions and the only safe attitude for her is facing the other way into the wind and sea. If she must go on downwind then a drogue to keep the stern into the wind becomes a necessity of life.

Staying Afloat

It would seem a sensible requirement of a yacht that no matter what disaster overtook her machinery or the normal integrity of her hull, she should stay afloat. Old-time ships built of wood very often did, to become derelicts which were once a considerable hazard about the oceans. The advent of steel construction and heavy engines made vessels basically unbuoyant – they sank when full of water. Now that in many ways hulls and machinery are becoming lighter it is possible again to consider seriously whether the basic vessel can be made buoyant. The arrival of plastics foams allows us to fill unused parts of the hull with almost pure buoyancy, and at 50 to 60 lb of buoyancy per cubic foot of foam it does not take too much to add up to floating the machinery. Hulls are usually just self-floating in wood or glass reinforced plastics. Perhaps the principal question is whether one does in fact want to go to the trouble. Very few craft are actually sunk at sea and the greater part of those that do sink are perhaps so antiquated as to have no real business in deep water. For these one suspects that a first-rate lifesaving set of dinghies, radios and flares would be for the general good all round.

The traditional answer to staying afloat in trouble is in the use of watertight bulkheads and some of the classification societies still require the fitting of collision bulkheads close to the ends of the vessel. These can be and are still used and fitted, but as yachts become smaller and more complex any really valuable system of watertight compartments, as far as staying afloat is concerned, becomes increasingly impracticable. Doors between compartments are the more necessary as the accommodation reaches an increasingly high density; and systems pipes and conduits have to run throughout and would require a trained crew to operate a battery of cocks to make watertight in an emergency. The principal use of many so-called watertight bulkheads seen in motor craft is to prevent the engine room spillage and smell extending through the owners' accommodation, or to stop a surge of bilge water to one end or other of the craft in a seaway.

It is a somewhat macabre process working out the effect of flooding in a yacht. To consider all the fine machinery and joinery work only for their underwater value requires a bit of a mental leap but is essential if the poor

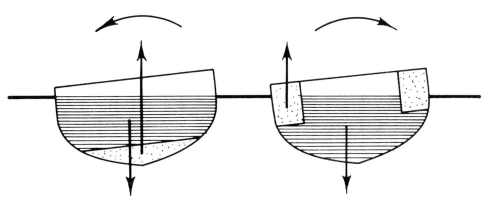

Fig. 14 Buoyancy placed too low can produce a capsizing moment in a craft full of water. Buoyancy placed in the right place can keep the craft stable and upright in a disaster.

owner is not to be further embarrassed in his emergency. The buoyancy has to be arranged so that the yacht will if possible settle level in the water and roll as little as possible. The vessel full of water has to be stable and able to cope with the free surface effects of the sea rolling from compartment to compartment. To keep the yacht level and stable the buoyancy material needs to be distributed all around the deck edge, and to keep it floating high it should be distributed through the bilges. As always in designing, a compromise is required with the buoyancy spread well about the hull and above the centre of gravity. In effect it should be placed at about half the height of the topsides throughout the length and high up in the ends.

In making the calculations or estimations for buoyancy the effect of any excessively self-buoyant hull or fitting features must be taken into effect. Bilge tanks can often provide a capsizing moment to be taken into effect. Yachts are sometimes overwhelmed by seas when they are lying momentarily on their sides. The buoyancy arrangements have to be such that she rights herself as she fills rather than capsizes.

Another modest and obvious point about foam buoyancy which is occasionally overlooked is that it is only of value while it is held in place. This not only refers to such elementary problems as happen to the capsized sailing dingy whose buoyancy bags are not secured and float away happily by themselves. In the greater loading of the buoyancy at work in a sizeable vessel the securing of decks and structures above the buoyancy has to be taken into account. Many elderly yachts are decked like pot lids held in place principally by gravity and a few modest fastenings. A good thrust from a buoyancy block would perhaps lift the deck, and if the buoyancy can escape you might as well not have bothered in the first place.

Apart from foam buoyancy there are other buoyancy materials available. One of the traditional materials is cork, although this is so surpassed by the artificial foam blocks and foamed in place buoyancy that it is now rarely seen. The same really applies to ping-pong balls, the record breaker's friend, for many vulnerable craft have been stuffed with these lightweight balls for security. Air bags are also to be seen. If they are kept inflated there is a chafe and maintenance problem and if they are kept uninflated ready for automatic inflation then someone has to put the automatic inflation into operation. The principal disadvantage of the foams lies in their weight, surprisingly enough. They weigh usually between 3 and 10 lb a cubic foot and therefore enough buoyancy to float an engine weighing a ton can amount to nearly 400 lb.

Sailing to Windward

Juan Baader
The Sailing Yacht
first published 1965

In 1962 Juan Baader, an Argentinian naval architect, wrote El Deporte de la Vela. *It was translated from the original Spanish into German, and thence into English, our edition being titled* The Sailing Yacht. *It is a masterful survey of the whole sport of sailing, in three parts: a technical exposition of how a boat sails, and the factors which affect performance; a survey of many of the different types of pleasure sailing boat in existence, and finally a description and brief history of the major sailing events throughout the world. In this extract, he outlines the factors affecting a yacht sailing to windward. The author writes:*

'*Many years ago, while I prepared myself to become a naval architect, my one desire was to design, and more than this, to build and sail yachts of all practical sizes. This was the dream of a young man who had designed his own 17-foot dinghy at the age of eighteen.*

'*My heart was always with sailing, but the design work that came in involved motor cruisers and utility motor craft, and led me to the situation some ten years later, where I owned my own boatyard in the Argentine. Gaining more experience, I wrote a book on motor cruisers and speed boats, explaining how to figure out speed and power of small- to medium-size power boats, say from 20–100 foot in length, pleasure craft as well as utility boats.*

'*I was always fascinated by propulsion by wind on sails, and it naturally occurred to me to find out if speed and power in sailing craft is accessible to mathematical investigation, and at the same time to attempt to explain it in easily understandable form. This gave the basic content to another book, titled in Spanish,* El Deporte de la Vela, *published in 1960 in the Argentine.*

'*The particular ability of modern sailing craft to make headway almost directly into the wind, was a phenomenon not clearly understood by even the most experienced sailors. Once a minor symposium on sails was held by a yachting magazine with assistance of four well-known sailmakers. During the discussion the chairman asked the sailmakers what forces made a boat sail almost into the wind, and they looked at each other and confessed that they really did not know. There were many erroneous explanations in circulation: even the theory of pressing a pumpkin seed between the finger-tips came closer to the truth than some of the information in sailing literature. This all happened years before Marchaj's book* Sailing Theory and Practice *appeared.*

'El Deporte de la Vela *was well received in Argentina and in Spanish-speaking countries, so that translations followed into the German, Dutch, English and Italian, in that order, and I hope that the popularity of its content may help many readers in their search for better understanding of sails and wind.*'

A yacht sailing close-hauled virtually *eats* its way into the wind. The fact that on this point of sailing any forward thrust can be extracted from the wind is quite remarkable. However, only a small part of the total wind force is accounted for by forward thrust. The greater part, on average three times as much, is converted into side force, which causes leeway and heeling. Heeling, in its turn, reduces the projected sail area.

Sails cannot be set without the necessary rigging consisting of mast, boom, halliards and sheets. The mast again needs to be stayed by shrouds, stays, spreaders, jumpers, etc. to help it take the wind pressure on the sail. All parts of the rigging are struck by the wind from almost ahead and thus cause a considerable part of the total wind resistance. Besides, the mast has an unfavourable influence on the sail by disturbing the air stream in exactly the place where it ought to strike the sail freely. All parts of the rigging, therefore, reduce the potential forward thrust of the sail and increase the heeling effect of the wind.

Every sail suffers a certain loss of efficiency when close-hauled, even if its cut is of the greatest perfection. The unavoidable twist in the upper part of the sail makes it necessary to sheet the sail in harder than is good for the lower part of the sail, so that *on average* the sail sets at the most efficient angle to the wind. To determine this angle, which has a decisive influence on the attainable speed, is largely a matter of the crew's skill.

As soon as the boat starts to heel, the centre of effort of all forward driving forces is no longer vertically over the boat's centreline but shifts to leeward. The thrust then acts on a lever arm outside the ship's centreline and therefore has a powerful luffing effect.

Despite these many disturbing influences, the boat makes its way through the water with astounding sureness and precision. It cannot even derive much benefit from the designed symmetrical shape of its hull, because a heeled hull is no longer symmetrical, and the water has to travel different distances to pass to windward and to leeward. Heeling always means increased resistance, but this is often compensated by an increase in the waterline length.

The side force of the wind causes *true* leeway. Boast with excessive lee or weather helm also make *false* leeway, which occurs as a result of the continued exaggerated angle of the rudder which is needed to hold a badly balanced boat on course. The angle of leeway in modern yachts is between 3° and 5°, but considerably larger angles may occur. Shallow-draught boats with a poor underwater profile and badly setting sails may have an angle of leeway of 10° or more when sailing to windward. While heeling increases the resistance due to the hull shape becoming asymmetrical, leeway causes a further significant increase in resistance which is called 'induced drag' and will be explained in a later chapter.

The lateral resistance of the hull, which counteracts leeway, can be imagined as being concentrated in the geometric centre of the hull. This,

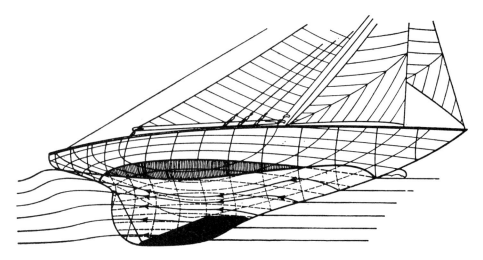

Fig. 15 The effect of the wind on a boat sailing to windward produces a threefold reaction in the hull: forward motion, heeling and leeway. Modern hull shapes are very efficient in converting the relatively small forward thrust into remarkable speeds and reducing leeway to a minimum, despite the fact that the side force is many times greater than the forward thrust.

the centre of lateral resistance (CLR for short) is always marked in the line drawings of a boat. In practice, however, the actual pressure centre, the dynamic CLR, lies forward of the geometric CLR. This is so because the fore body of the hull cuts through undisturbed water, which resists leeward drift more than the disturbed water through which the after body moves.

Similarly complicated rules apply to the sails. Here, too, the dynamic centre of effort does not coincide with the geometric CE, because the forward parts of the sail are subject to greater wind pressure than the after parts. Thus, both centres, the CLR of the hull and the CE of the sail area, lie forward of the geometric centres. It would seem, then, that to result in a balanced boat the CE should lie vertically above the CLR. Unfortunately, though, even if the two centres were to lie in the same vertical plane (and, as yet, no way has been found to calculate their position accurately), a balance of forces cannot be achieved because, due to heeling, the thrust acts from a point *far outboard* and has a considerable luffing effect. One might imagine that the boat was not being pulled along by the bow, but by a tow line attached to a boom sticking out over the side. It is obvious that this method of towing can only be compensated for by angling the rudder. The luffing effect of the thrust lever becomes stronger as the boat heels over. If the centre of effort of the sail area is moved forward some appreciable distance, an opposite falling-off moment can be obtained, which counterbalances the luffing moment at an average angle of heel. It is, of course, not possible to consider and counterbalance all angles of heel when determining the position of the centre of effort, merely an average angle.

In conclusion it must be added that the part of the hull which is above the water is also exposed to the wind and therefore causes air friction, which is most detrimental on the wind.

In Fig. 16 some of the things which occur in sailing to windward have been shown in diagrammatic form. It is assumed that the yacht sails at an angle of 45° to the true wind, which is well within the abilities of any modern sailing keelboat or dinghy. Under ideal racing conditions, some boats can get as close as 39° to the true wind. In the case of Fig. 16 average conditions have been assumed, with a wind speed of approximately 10 knots, in which non-planing types of boats already reach 90 per cent of their maximum speed. The apparent wind, shown by the arrow on the left, is much stronger than the true wind, indicated by the arrow on the right. At 45° to the true wind (which cannot be established from on board) the course sailed in relation to the apparent wind is 27°. If the mark lies dead to windward, which means the yacht will be tacking, 70 per cent of her speed through the water will be *speed made good*, which means speed, or way, into the wind.

In 1936 a scientifically measured series of experiments was conducted by the then head of the Stevens Institute of Technology, K S M Davidson.

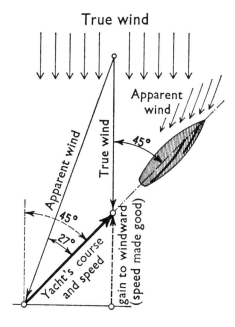

Fig. 16 Most modern boats can sail as close as 45° to the true wind. In this case the distance made good to windward is 70 per cent of the actual distance.

The yacht used in the experiment was *Gimcrack*, a newly designed type of racing yacht similar to a 6-metre. An experienced and particularly skilled helmsman sailed her close-hauled in all winds, while all measurable values were recorded. The results were used in comparison with test data obtained with models, which were just then assuming increased importance in yacht tests. The results of these test runs became known as the 'Gimcrack-coefficients'. Since *Gimcrack* is not a widely known type, the figures have been adapted by the author to fit the internationally known Dragon class and are presented in diagrammatic form in Figs. 17 to 21.

The first of these graphs, Fig. 17, explains the relationship between speed and angle of heel, sailing on the wind. Even light winds, which cause the boat to heel only very slightly, give it an appreciable turn of speed. With an angle of heel of only 5° the boat already reaches half its maximum speed. At 11° of heel a speed of 4 knots is reached. As the wind increases so does the angle of heel, but the speed only increases by a very small amount after this and reaches its maximum, 5·1 knots, at 30° of heel. If the wind increases further, the boat will continue to heel further, but the speed will then *decrease* rather than increase.

The next graph, Fig. 18, illustrates the total resistance at these speeds, at the same time showing the corresponding angles of heel. The dotted line shows what would happen if the boat was sailing upright and making no leeway. It can again be seen that at 11° of heel a speed of 4 knots is reached, and at the same time the total resistance can be read off: 30 lb (14 kg). At 30° of heel and a speed of 5·1 knots the total resistance is considerably greater: 82 lb (37 kg). As the angle of heel increases, so does the resistance. At an angle of heel of 40° the resistance rises to 110 lb (50 kg), but the thrust obtained from the sails does not increase at the same rate so that the speed actually *decreases*. The difference between the dotted line for the boat sailing upright and the bold line for the boat sailing heeled illustrates the important effect of heeling (which upsets the symmetry of the hull) and leeway (which causes induced drag).

In the two first graphs wind speed is not indicated. Figure 19 shows all the previous figures in relation to wind speeds. In a 10-knot wind, for example, a Dragon will sail at an angle of heel of 20° and reach a speed of 4·8 knots. Once again it can be seen that the maximum speed is reached at an angle of heel of approximately 30°, which is related to a wind speed of 14·5 knots. With increasing wind speeds, the boat's speed does not increase any more and eventually decreases. The lower, dotted curve shows the speed made good, i.e. the actual way gained directly into the wind. The fact that this speed is as high as it is amounts virtually to a miracle and is due only to the excellent windward qualities of hull and rig.

The fourth in this series of graphs, Fig. 20 illustrates the effect of the wind most clearly. The bold curve shows that the apparent wind is always much faster than the true wind. A true wind of 16 ft/sec (nearly 10 knots),

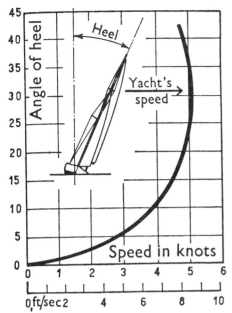

Fig. 17 This graph, which shows the speed and angles of heel of a Dragon, was drawn up with reference to the experimental runs of the yacht *Gimcrack*. It can be seen that the greatest speed is reached at 32° of heel. As the wind force and the angle of heel increase further, the speed drops.

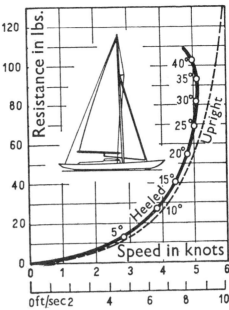

Fig. 18 Resistance to forward motion in a Dragon in relation to speed and angle of heel. The broken curve shows the resistance of the upright hull. The difference between the two curves shows the detrimental influence of heeling and leeway.

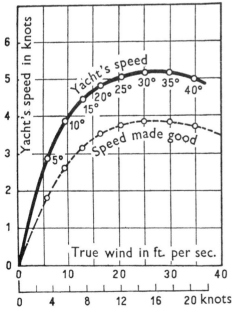

Fig. 19 The speed and distance made good to windward of a Dragon in relation to the true wind. Angles of heel are given as parameters.

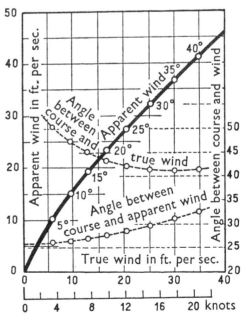

Fig. 20 Three curves pertaining to a Dragon sailing on the wind, indicating the speed of the apparent wind in relation to the true wind and the angles between course sailed and true and apparent wind respectively.

for example, is turned by the speed of the boat itself into an apparent wind of 21·5 ft/sec (nearly 13 knots).

The upper, dotted curve is of special interest. It indicates the angle between course and true wind and shows that the exceptionally narrow angle of 39°, which we mentioned earlier, was never reached in this case. The smallest angle attained by the boat was 42° at a wind speed of over 14·5 knots. At first sight it seems illogical that the boat cannot get as close to the wind in light airs, but this is a logical consequence of the fact that in light winds the boat already reaches a relatively high speed in comparison to the true wind and thereby makes the apparent wind *draw ahead* quite considerably.

The last diagram, Fig. 21, illustrates both the boat's speed through the water and the speed made good in relation to the true wind. The bold curve on top shows that even in the lightest of winds the boat never reaches the speed of the wind itself, which is hardly surprising. But it comes close

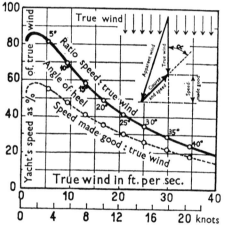

Fig. 21 The bold curve indicates the speed of the Dragon on the wind in relation to true wind. In light winds the boat reaches speeds of over 80 per cent of the true wind speed. In strong winds the speed drops to about 20 per cent of the true wind speed. The broken line represents the speed made good to windward in relation to the true wind.

to it. In a light breeze of about 2 knots the Dragon reaches 85 per cent of the true wind speed. In a pleasant sailing breeze of about 10 knots the boat sails at just half the wind speed. The dotted line shows the *speed made good* to windward in relation to the true wind speed. At the same wind speed of 10 knots the Dragon's speed made good is 36 per cent of the speed of the true wind.

These Gimcrack-coefficients illustrate convincingly the wonderful ability of the modern yacht to cheat the wind into propelling it at remarkable speeds into the very wind itself.

The Race is not to the Swift

Knut Krieger

This piece was published in Britain in Yachts and Yachting *in May 1976. Sadly, the author, an American chemistry professor, is now dead, but his wife writes as follows: 'You asked how Knut came to write* The Race is not to the Swift. *He loved sailing, and for eleven years spent every minute he could spare from his work sailing the Chesapeake Bay in his sloop,* Ailuros. *When he wasn't actually sailing, I suspect he was thinking about it. He said that one evening while doodling with a pair of compasses he came across "a remarkable paradox", and that's how it started.'*

Knut Krieger, in his exposition of this 'remarkable paradox', gives his own version of the limiting factors on a yacht's performance to windward.

Every sailor knows that as boat speed increases the apparent wind moves further forward. Probably he also knows that this fact is expressed quantitatively in the statement true wind vector = apparent wind vector + boat speed vector.

This equation gives rise to the familiar vector diagram of Fig. 22.

Every sailor knows also, to his sorrow, that he cannot sail closer to the apparent wind than some fixed angle. To be sure this angle varies with the design of the boat, the cut of the sails, the care which the skipper has taken in tuning, the state of wind and water, and perhaps other factors known only to God and Olympic helmsmen. But to develop our argument, let us assume that in your case this minimum angle is 45°.

Now let us look at a common situation, illustrated in Fig. 23. You, master under God of the ship 'Walloper', are at point S. The true wind vector, T, is exactly contrary. Obviously you must sail close-hauled. For the sake of geometrical simplicity, let us assume that your boat speed, B_w, is equal to the true wind speed, and that you start on the starboard tack. You can easily convince yourself that B_w and T form two sides of a right

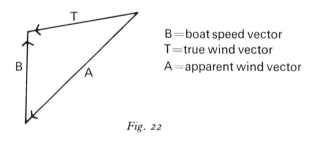

B = boat speed vector
T = true wind vector
A = apparent wind vector

Fig. 22

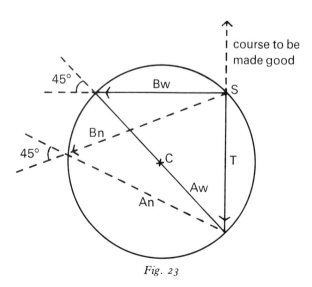

Fig. 23

isosceles triangle whose hypotenuse is A_w, the apparent wind speed. Not that the angle between B_w and A_w is 45°, as it must be since you can sail no closer to the apparent wind than 45°. Note also that under these conditions the speed made good is exactly zero, since you are sailing at right angles to the course to be made good.

To carry the argument to its logical (and paradoxical) conclusion, we need a little more geometry. The triangle formed by B_w, T, and A_w can be inscribed in a circle whose centre is at C, the midpoint of the apparent wind vector, A_w. It is a property of inscribed angles (don't blame me – blame Euclid) that if T is fixed and the angle between B_w and A_w is fixed every possible position that a boat of any speed could reach in unit time (1 hour if B_w and T are in knots) – assuming T is constant and the tacking angle is 45° – lies on this circle. If you have forgotten this property of inscribed angles, check with your favourite schoolboy – or girl – who will not only confirm it but prove it.

Once this elementary fact is grasped, the horrid conclusions follow inexorably. Some of these conclusions are illustrated by the following examples:

1. Your friend (enemy?), master of 'Nimbleheels', with whom you occasionally race informally, has by diligent attention to the seamanlike arts so tuned his boat that under these conditions his speed is greater than yours although he can point no higher. Now draw on Fig. 23 the dotted line of the boat speed vector for 'Nimbleheels', B_n. Since B_n is greater than B_w, 'Nimbleheels' sees the apparent wind vector A_n, intersects the circle at a point downwind of S, and actually loses ground along the course to be made good. Behold the rewards of virtue.

2. On the other hand, the master of 'Sluggard' typically allows whiskers two feet long to grow on his hull. The result is that the speed of 'Sluggard' is only about half that of your boat. I leave you to show for yourself that 'Sluggard' will beat you upwind every time. Such are the wages of sin.

Obviously there is an optimum boat speed which will produce the maximum speed made good. A little exercise in trigonometry (which is good for you) will show that if the minimum tacking angle is 45° this speed is:

$$B = 0.54 \text{ T}$$

and that if the boat speed is 0.54 T the speed made good will be a maximum, namely,

$$\text{speed made good} = 0.21 \text{ T}$$

A little more exercise in trigonometry (which is even better for you) will enable you to calculate x in the equation for optimum boat speed:

$$B = xT$$

and y in the equation:

$$\text{speed made good} = yT$$

for the tacking angle characteristic of any boat.

If you care to check your trigonometry, the answers are:

$$x = \frac{1}{\sqrt{2}} \quad \frac{\cos\frac{t}{2} - \sin\frac{t}{2}}{\sin t}; \quad y = \frac{1 - \sin t}{2 \sin t}$$

where t is the tacking angle.

Of course, if you are determined to resist education you can consult the table, which gives the value of x and y for several tacking angles, t.

Table			
t (degrees)	x	y	Notes
10	3·70	2·38	
15	2·35	1·43	
20	1·68	0·96	
25	1·32	0·73	
30	1·00	0·50	'Pincher' optimum
35	0·80	0·37	
40	0·66	0·28	
45	0·54	0·21	'Walloper' optimum
50	0·45	0·15	
55	0·37	0·11	

Consulting the table, you will readily see how that devil, the master of 'Pincher', who has contrived with more than mortal guile to reduce his tacking angle to 30° while maintaining his speed the same as yours, manages to go upwind like a fiend while 'Walloper' gets nowhere at all.

You can see also that, even after you have learned to choose the optimum conditions for 'Walloper', 'Pincher' will go upwind more than twice as fast as 'Walloper'

$$\left(\frac{0\cdot50}{0\cdot21} = 2\cdot4\right).$$

And the moral of this is: pinch, brothers, pinch; but pinch with care.

In the event that the wind is not *exactly* contrary – a rare event so far as the author's personal experience goes – the table above can still be used. In this case the table is entered with (t−w) instead of t on the favourable (making) tack. Here w is the acute angle between the course to be made good and the direction of the true wind.

On the unfavourable tack the table is entered with (t + w) instead of t. In both cases the values of x and y give, respectively, the optimum boat speed and speed made good on each tack.

So much for the wonders of geometry. Now for practical applications. It is obvious by now that if your boat speed is too high you cannot sail upwind and that to maximise speed made good to windward boat speed must be nicely adjusted to your minimum tacking angle.

Thus the advice to the fast sailor going upwind must be: *tow a bucket over the stern*. Naturally it must be an *adjustable* bucket (patent applied for) so that the necessary fine adjustment of B can be made.

If this sage advice is followed, it appears to the author that any of the following results may ensue: (1) You win the race and are considered a magician. (2) You manage to lose anyway and are committed to the funny farm. (3) Some combination of (1) and (2). (4) The opposition is so psyched out by this remarkable spectacle that they make egregious errors and lose disgracefully.

Racing: Techniques

Winning without Magic

Eric Twiname
Start To Win
first published 1973

Start To Win *is a refreshingly readable book on the approach to racing: it has been highly successful since it was published in 1973. The author writes:*

'"*Why don't you do a book on racing tactics?" they asked me.*

'"*It's been done," I replied naïvely, unaware of how publishers function. "There are too many books on it already. There can't be anything more to say." It turned out, when I had a close look at what had been written, that there was.*

'*World champions had told all (or nearly all) about what made them win, but that wasn't necessarily any good to the middle of the fleet sailor who couldn't tell a good windshift when he saw one. Journalists with an eye on the needs of their potential readers had written readable and useful books, but only to a certain level, since they themselves had not achieved the heights of racing success.*

'*Not that I had; but I strove to make amends for the considerable handicap of never having won a world championship or an Olympic medal by, metaphorically, starting at the other end of the line. I began by finding out why all those vast numbers of people who race and lose do their losing. I crewed for them, I watched them, I listened to them in the bar.*

'*What did they know that would enable them to improve easily, quickly and efficiently? As simply, methodically and entertainingly as I could give it, the answer was my book,* Start To Win.

'*In any substantial piece of writing, unless you're inordinately lucky, there comes a time when you know you've nearly got it right, but not quite. This happened when I thought I'd finished the manuscript, which still carried its horribly dull working title,* Winning Tactics.

'*Much of it I was happy with, but the whole just didn't gel. Everyone else seemed happy enough, but I wasn't. Nor, fortunately, was Nigel Redfern, a Cumbrian friend whose then considerable race-losing skills I had studied during the writing of the book.*

'*The title, he agreed, was awful. The other thing wrong was the first chapter. Then, for as long as it takes to get through a bottle of sherry slowly, Nigel, his wife Margaret and I threw possible titles back and forth, until all other possibilities fell by the wayside and we were left with* Start To Win.

'*Armed with a title I was actually excited about, the first chapter virtually re-wrote itself, and after Bill Banks had rounded off the photography with an excellent series of Laser pictures, including the jacket shot, the whole thing suddenly felt completely right. Five years later it still does.*

'*No piece of work has ever given me as much pleasure, both in the writing and from the enjoyment people have had from it. Nor can any writer be more highly rewarded than by the unsolicited thanks of readers who have been helped by his book. And the warmth of gratitude I have received from complete strangers at sailing clubs in different parts of the world for producing this one surely outweighs the more measurable rewards I have banked. The first chapter is the essence of a book which was nothing less than a labour of love.*'

Start To Win is written for the benefit of ordinary helmsmen who may never race in the Olympics but do want to win their club races and perhaps one day their national championships. So emphasis is all the time on the skills and thinking of the man at the helm and his crew. In an age of technical wizardry there is always the let-out that we're being beaten because the top man has better sails, mast, hull and equipment, when in fact he is a better helmsman who knows precisely what to do to get any boat round the course as fast as ever it will go. The race-winning tactics and ideas included here are not therefore limited to a few specialised classes; they apply to any dinghy that relies on crew weight for ballast.

Some experts would have you believe that reducing a boat's weight by throwing shackles over the side, or by a helmsman living on the right diet, becoming a gymnast and finding the right dust-proof room in which to apply the twelfth coat of paint on the hull were the things that made the difference between winning and losing. Certainly this kind of detail may make the difference between first and fifth place at the Olympics. But the vast majority of helmsmen who race do not devote most of their waking hours to sailing and it is misleading to suggest that for a club sailor these are points that matter.

The helming-to-win diagram forms the basis of the book. A helmsman can only make decisions about one thing at once, so to make the all-important tactical decisions he has to switch off his conscious fast sailing side and rely on automatic skills. The earlier chapters explain how to build up these automatic skills so that they can be relied on, and how to develop the fast sailing skills that make winning look easy.

The two most important sides of tactics – choosing the fastest route round the course in relation to the natural conditions and avoiding the slowing influence of other boats – are covered in the middle of the book. In the final part there is a rules guide designed to make it easy for anyone to interpret quickly almost any incident to which the rules apply. So much for the menu. To make the main courses more easily digestible, we should now consider the attitude of mind that enables some helmsmen consistently to win.

The only secret of winning is that there isn't one – not a single mystical explanation anyway. The pinnacle of sailing success is supported by a vast pyramid of often quite small pieces of sailing knowledge, each one perfectly applied. A good helmsman's boat is well tuned but, much more important, he himself is tuned to win. And just as boat tune depends on getting even small details right, successful helmsmanship relies more than anything on perfecting even the most trivial-seeming techniques of sailing and combining these into a near-flawless racing ability.

Obviously there are certain things a successful helmsman does that con-tribute more to his success than others. Working windshifts well on the windward legs, for example, is at least twenty times as important as adjust-

First-place thinking

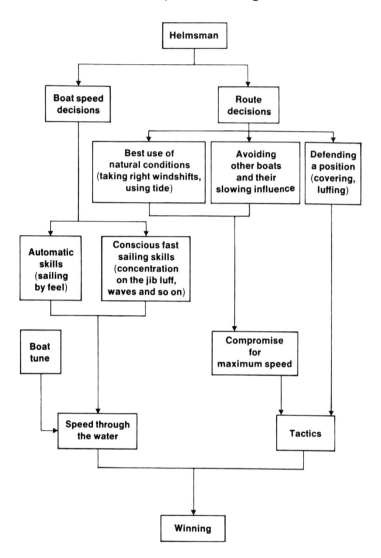

Fig. 24 A race is won on a series of decisions correctly made. When concentrating on the tactical side of fast sailing (the route decisions) the helmsman has to rely heavily on his automatic skills: he cannot, for example, concentrate on approaching gusts and watch the jib luff at the same time. On sea courses top helmsmen will spend three-quarters of his time on the conscious fast sailing skills and only a quarter on making route decisions. On inland waters he will spend more than half his time working out the tactics that ensure he takes the fastest route round the course. In general, the left hand side of the diagram is more important on the sea, and the right (plus automatic skills) more important on inland waters.

ing the centreboard correctly downwind; holding the boat within five degrees of the upright position all the time in heavy weather is a hundred times more important than adjusting the mainsail's outhaul tension correctly in the same conditions.

Olympic medallists get all these things right nearly all the time. The average club helmsman gets many of them wrong all the time – wrong enough usually to keep him out of the prizes.

If you can spot windshifts and you sail on inland waters, the minutiae of boat tune will be as near irrelevant as makes no difference. In winning races there are therefore some things which are vitally important and some which should be given a much lower priority. Some knowledge of these priorities is essential for anyone who wants to improve his sailing quickly. My own experience is that if you do nothing more than rearrange in a tail-ender's mind the importance he should attribute to individual items (like jib sheet trim, mainsail luff lifting, heeling, prediction of windshifts and so on) he immediately stops being a tail-ender.

If that seems a rash statement, test it next time you are ashore when a race is being sailed in anything over force 3. Wait till the boats are on the second beat and ask someone who knows nothing about sailing what differences he can see in the way the boats at the front are sailing compared with those at the back. After a few facetious replies like 'faster', he will point out that the boats at the front are sailing more upright than those at the back.

Nothing unusual or remarkable about that – the phenomenon is universal: dinghies at the front of fleets tend to sail upright in heavy weather, those at the back heel. So now we can ask ourselves why do the helmsmen at the back persist in heeling when the advantages of sailing upright are obvious, even to a non-sailor on the shore?

I have from time to time asked some of the tail-enders and the usual answer is: 'We're not heavy enough to hold her up, although we *were* trying to.'

A fair enough answer until you find that a lighter crew who finished up front were holding their boat upright. Further questioning of the tail-ender will reveal that he was trying to get as much speed upwind as possible by keeping the sails full all the time.

And this is where he has his priorities wrong. Common sense or a book has told him that to get the most speed out of the boat the sails should be kept full and driving. Quite right for most conditions, but keep the sails driving in heavy weather and the boat lays over on her ear. He knows that she shouldn't do this, but if the sails are full and driving, he argues, surely that's what matters. The non-sailor on the shore could have told him that it is not. The first priority in heavy weather dinghy sailing is to keep the boat upright, whatever that takes. Once the back marker develops his heavy weather technique with that priority impressed in his mind, he will no longer flounder along, counting his finishing positions from the back.

That was a simple example and I could give many others, but it illustrates the point that a mistaken order of priorities is a handicap that most helmsmen carry when they start to race. The sooner they can sort out what matters most at any moment in a race, the sooner they will start to win. This book is laid out with those priorities clearly in mind, so that while mast rake receives maybe a quarter of a page, mark rounding gets a whole chapter and windshifts over twenty pages. There are no detailed analyses of rules by number; there is instead a rule section designed to answer directly the relevant question 'Will I be in the right in this situation?' or afterwards, 'Was I in the right?'

Although there is an important physical side to helming, races are primarily won in the mind. This is so because except in the most extreme heavy weather the physical side of the game doesn't demand the same co-ordination and reaction that, say, squash demands. (If it did, we would all be noticeably better on one tack than the other.)

Nevertheless, the physical business of making a sailing boat move through the water in the best direction at its greatest speed requires full time attention, leaving no available thinking time for selecting the ideal moments to tack or even to look around at the positions of other boats. And yet to reach the front of a competitive fleet you have to use the natural elements to the best possible advantage and weave the least wasteful path through the rest of the fleet. So here is the fundamental priority crisis: tactics or boat speed. Understanding exactly how expert helmsmen resolve this conflict throughout their races will take us as near as we'll ever get to the secret of winning.

Aircraft pilots switch on an automatic pilot whenever they want to attend to something other than keeping their aeroplane on course. And this is essentially what a racing helmsman must do. The helmsman's automatic pilot isn't electronic of course; it relies on senses like balance, the feel of the boat and a sense of the direction of his boat, even when he's looking elsewhere.

Now this automatic pilot skill may sound fanciful, a convenient figment of my imagination, something beyond the reach of an ordinary helmsman. In fact it's none of these things. If you try sailing in medium weather one day with your eyes closed you'll appreciate what I mean. You'll find that you have to rely on senses you may not previously even have been aware of using – the feel of the wind on your head, the angle of heel of the boat, the pressure on your hand holding the tiller, the sound of the bow wave and the changing of the wind noises in the sails and rigging as you head up too far or bear away too much. To be able to sail without using your eyes at all is therefore excellent practice and an important skill. My own estimate is that for a middle-of-the-fleet helmsman, performance will be improved ten times as much by sailing blind for a couple of hours than by the most efficient use of two hours spent boat tuning.

The expert can switch his automatic pilot ability on and off as he wants. He loses 1 or 2 per cent in speed with his automatic pilot in operation, so he uses it sparingly except in situations where he'll lose 10 or 20 per cent by not using it at all. The skill isn't only useful to him as he looks around to see what's going on about him; it is important to a lesser extent as he concentrates on the fast sailing of his boat. He operates as a kind of machine minder: he looks carefully at how his boat is sailing most of the time, but only need concentrate all his thinking on the boat handling when something has to change – like during a gybe or when the wind drops and the sheets need easing.

On inland water more tactical decisions crop up than on long sea courses, which means that the automatic pilot skill matters most of all on lakes, estuaries and rivers. More is likely to hang on a single decision on a long sea course, but fewer decisions are necessary, so more time can be spent trying to squeeze that extra bit of speed out of the boat. The proportion of time during a race spent on thinking tactics on inland water has to be around 75 per cent on the windward legs; on the sea the proportion is more like 30 per cent. During most of this time the automatic pilot will be of the 'machine minder' style, but for important periods the boat will be, as it were, on full automatic pilot.

Because the race-winning helmsman has developed this automatic skill to a high degree, his boat demands less of his attention and he can spend more of the race than can his less skilled opponents in thinking about and planning his tactics. In coaching sessions covered by video tape recorders, even quite good helmsmen see themselves on the playback throwing away half a length of windward ground during a five-second glance over the shoulder.

Some helmsman–crew partnerships actually split the helming role down the middle: the fast sailing part is left to the helmsman, while the crew decides on the best route to sail. In a boat where the crew hasn't much else to do this arrangement can work well provided his tactics are good.

When the crew's tactics are flawless an average helmsman's performance can improve spectacularly. I could give many examples of the back-of-the-fleet helmsman finding himself at the front because he was being crewed by an expert helmsman who dictated which route they took round the course. In a medium weather Firefly race recently a helmsman in his first season's racing managed fourth place in a highly competitive fleet of twenty with a pundit helmsman as crew. The boat's usual place was last.

This also supports the idea that winning is, except in the heaviest weather, a mental rather than a physical problem. Put the right ideas in the mind of the inexperienced helmsman and he can win, although in heavy weather he'll also need the right set of reflexes.

All helmsmen develop their skills more slowly than they would like to and most improve more slowly than they might. The main problem is that they have to learn twice. To start with the important thing is to be able to handle the boat and get round the course without hitting anything or capsizing. In learning how to do that a future racing helmsman learns many of the basics well enough to get him by, but nothing like well enough to win races. Yet his ways of doing things become habit, and as his self-taught techniques are inefficient as racing tools they have to be unlearnt first before they can be re-learned in a way that will enable him to win races. Many helmsmen never go through this un-learning and re-learning process and they stay half-way down the fleet, making the same mistakes at the same marks in the same boat year in, year out.

It often puzzled me that some helmsmen seem incapable of seeing their own mistakes or even recognising the consequences of them. What happens is that they don't sail looking for mistakes to correct in their own technique; they tend to attribute their defeat to the expert's excellence rather than their own inadequacies.

The man who wins has looked hard and long for the inadequacies in his own technique and tactical skill and got rid of them, for there was a time when he sailed as badly as the worst helmsmen behind him.

The consistent middle-of-the-fleet man prefers not to think of the inadequacies in his own technique – not in any detailed way – because it's more comfortable, less trouble, to accept a lowly position and attribute the success of others to their superior boats, to some mystical secret the top men possess, and sometimes even to luck. As long as the middle-of-the-fleet man thinks like that he'll continue to be consistently and thoroughly beaten.

The non-sailor watching the close-hauled dinghies was questioned in a way that made him look for differences between the handling of the leading boats, compared with the tail-enders. And merely by looking at a race in a way that a helmsman closely involved could not see it, the observer could draw the conclusion that sailing a dinghy upright in heavy weather wins races. If he continued his observation more closely from a launch, he would be able to see precisely how the race-winner was able to keep his boat upright, while the tail-ender was not.

Put the tail-ender in the shoes of questioning observer of a race and he can – provided he deliberately goes out to ask himself questions – see and learn more than he would in ten races. But watching is not necessarily seeing. The non-sailor could see things a middle-of-the-fleet man could not because the middle-of-the-fleet man would only see what he wanted to see, while the non-sailor would rely solely on the evidence of his eyes. The middle-of-the-fleet man would instinctively relate what he saw to his own technique, so that heeling at the back of the fleet would be explained rather than criticised. ('It's too strong to hold the boat up, I know that problem.') Whereas the attitude to what he sees that will lead him in a race-winning direction is: 'It obviously doesn't pay to let the boat heel since the man at the back does and the man at the front doesn't. What, exactly, are the two helmsmen doing differently?' If he answers that question, which he can by watching closely, he can un-learn his own wrong methods and learn the right ones.

Children are particularly good at learning because they play about in boats, deliberately trying stupid things for the hell of it, and in the process find out about how to handle their boats. In doing show-off capsizes in force 2, they learn what makes a boat capsize and therefore what to avoid doing in a force 6 if they're to stay upright. So through playing, children do their un-learning as they go along.

As a method of improving quickly I would suggest deliberately trying to do everything worse than usual (particularly tacking, mark-rounding and so on) so you learn the wrong ways of doing things. The right ways then become more obvious and more precisely defined. For anyone who has never tried it, sailing without a rudder is an eye-opener. There's more to be learnt in an hour about boat handling in this way than in a season of flogging round the marks.

One of the problems with relying on club racing as a means to improve helming skill is that you're inclined to get into tactical routines; it's very easy to get into bad habits. One side of the beat becomes your favourite. It may be the best one, but if you don't occasionally experiment with the other, you can't be certain. It's easy to become (or remain) immune to windshifts; it's easy to change nothing, just do everything the same as usual. And if you don't win, that means – as I don't hesitate to repeat – doing some of these things wrong all the time. Yet experiment is not likely to immediately improve your position – first you'll do worse. So the tendency is not to experiment during a race, and improvement comes very slowly, if at all.

Golfers, cricketers and athletes practise to improve their play. For some reason, few racing helmsmen seem to bother; yet by doing a little sailing practice you can pick up more boat speed than by simply flogging round the buoys yet again. Tacking, for example, is often regarded as an irritating break between racing on port and racing on starboard, but it is itself part of the race and it can be done wastefully or well. To learn during a race how to do a roll tack would mean tacking worse than usual to start with, so most people don't attempt it. But outside races, when there's nothing to worry about except the quality of the tack, you can experiment with every imaginable variation: settle for the most efficient and taking improves. The same goes for gybing, mark-rounding, windward technique and any other sailing skill.

So far I have not mentioned boat tune. Again this is for reason of priority. There is a trend at present towards complication and complexity and a fetish that demands everything on the boat be adjustable. We have adjustable diamond tensioners, hydraulic shroud adjusters, cockpits full of coloured control lines running to banks of jamming cleats, screw-operated mast rams and everything except (so far) instantly variable hull shapes.

In this welter of technology gone mad the one variable that matters most of all tends to be forgotten– the human beings sailing the machine. I'm not for a moment suggesting that boat tune isn't important, but for club racing it is vastly over-rated as a race winning factor. At the Olympic level boat tune, even one superior sail, can make the difference between helmsmen who are themselves of almost equal ability. At club level helming ability is the big variable – a perfect set of sails trimmed wrongly will move a boat appreciably more slowly than an average set trimmed correctly.

If you suspect your boat of letting you down, persuade a friend whose boat is known to be good to swap with you for a race or two. A noticeable improvement in your finishing position would mean that the boat was to blame; an unchanged finishing position would mean it wasn't.

As I am primarily a sailor of one-design dinghies, I have probably been able to study the differences in helming techniques and skills more closely than I could in a restricted class. And since virtually all of Britain's leading dinghy helmsmen started in one-design dinghies, I can only conclude that in developing race-winning skills the priority should be helming skill first, boat tune second. The more highly developed your helming skill, the more significant boat tune becomes. John Oakeley in his book *Winning* and Fletcher and Ross in *Tuning a Sailing Yacht* deal with tuning in more detail and with more authority than I could bring to it, so if you want to get the finer points of tuning right, read one of these books.

To summarise, then, a winning approach to racing is a questioning, critical one. The helmsmen who excuse themselves for consistently indifferent performances will always perform indifferently; those who attack their own sailing technique critically and experimentally will improve, and improve quickly.

Ocean Racing Strategy

John Illingworth
Offshore/Further Offshore
first published 1949

As K Adlard Coles says in his Foreword, it was John Illingworth's Offshore *which really established Adlard Coles Limited, both financially and in the way of setting standards of authority to be maintained. Originally published in 1949, the book was regularly revised to keep pace with the rapid development of ocean racing. Illingworth renamed the book* Further Offshore *in 1969. Through all the updating and revising, the following chapter on strategy required little change. The author writes: 'I wrote the first* Offshore *at the instigation of Adlard Coles who persuaded me that what I had to say would be of interest and help to my fellow yachtsmen. I imagine that the task of choosing one's favourite extract from his own writings presents any author with a very difficult choice, but my reasons for choosing Chapter VI of* Further Offshore *were very simple. There have been fewer words written on the strategy of ocean racing than on any other aspect of this sport. It pleases me to think that, having written this chapter many many years ago, in fact, the thoughts and views on the subject I held then have stood the test of time and are still valid today.'*

Covering Rival Boats

Unlike considerations applying to regatta sailing, a lot of one's actions off shore do not deal with or concern the other competing yachts, because in most cases there will be a number of competing yachts, anything from six to one hundred and forty. In many cases they will be sailing widely different courses and it is not as a rule politic to concentrate on covering a particular boat; not unless you are convinced she is your most dangerous rival or that in covering her you are not going appreciably out of your way.

In class racing, without time allowance, covering usually consists of keeping between your rival and the mark. In ocean racing if you rate a little lower than the rival in question you may be able to cover him by dogging his course, so to speak. But if it is leading you into courses of which you do not approve – getting you too much to windward or to leeward perhaps – then it should not as a rule be continued, that is, unless you are near the finish; because although you may be holding your bigger rival nicely at the moment, a change in conditions later – such as a strengthening wind – may enable him to slip away and save his time under the changed conditions.

Maintaining Speed rather than Course

Before we pass on to consider the policy for various points of sailing, there is a point we must make in a general way about sailing towards one's mark. Though naturally the direct course is a thing one must have clearly in mind, don't let's get bound to it. It is far more important to keep the boat sailing at a good speed towards a distant mark, pointing somewhere in the neighbourhood of the right direction, than to pinch on to the exact course and have the yacht doing a lot less than her best.

When sailing off to gain speed, the extra distance one travels, always speaking of making for a turning point off shore and a real stretch ahead of you, is much less than one might at first sight imagine. We will examine this in more detail later. Meanwhile we can say that the all but golden tactical rule is 'keep her moving regardless of the exact course'.

If you as skipper, or navigator, find your crew are badly inflicted with 'Rhumb Line Phobia', one of the childish but partially effective dodges is never to draw the complete rhumb line on the chart – simply plot one D.R. position and read off one's course ordered and note it in the log. Be very clear that I am not advocating any relaxation in the navigation or plotting; I am simply suggesting that the hard black line – that prudish path from which we may fear to wander – is sometimes a false guide.

Ever Changing Rhumb Line

To take the matter a stage farther; to drive the spike well home as it were; consider this aspect. The rhumb line is the direct course between your last mark and your next. But with the tides, and maybe the necessity to steer off to keep up one's best speed, or to take a board on the wind which carries you off to one side or the other, with these things and others one is often going to get off the line. And as soon as you are appreciably off the line it ceases to have real significance, except for its academic value subsequently. What should interest you as skipper, or mate, is the new direct course from your present position to the next mark. The quickest way to the next mark becomes a problem in which one's previous direct courses are of no consequence. Very obvious you may say, and so it is when one sits down here to analyse it calmly. But just the same there are many cases on record where boats have painfully worked their way back on to the original rhumb line, as though it was some lovely smooth path.

There is, it is needless perhaps to say, another extreme; one can overdo the business of sailing off to find the fastest points of sailing; particularly in fresh conditions. Talking to other skippers after the 1945–6 Hobart Race I was under the distinct impression that most of them had on that occasion altered course an unnecessary amount with a view to working wind and set to the best advantage. The Australian yachtsmen are very speed-minded – and perhaps less navigation-minded than most of us in the old country. This was confirmed when the various track charts were superimposed. The breezes, apart from the gale period with wind from ahead, were mostly moderate to fresh commanding ones and our distance sailed was a good deal less than most. I fancy it was partly on this account that we managed to establish a big lead on *Winston Churchill,* who was just behind us when we cleared the New South Wales Coast, and a good deal bigger and faster than *Rani.*

Correcting for Tide

One's navigation manuals teach one to correct one's course for tide. And if one is likely to cross the area in question within the space of one flood or one ebb one must lay one's course corrected accordingly. But should the job involve crossing one or more complete tides it is quite important to make an overall plan. Supposing a crossing from the Sovereign light-vessel off Beachy Head to the Le Havre lightship – which is part of the famous R.O.R.C. Channel Race – takes one flood and one ebb, it is far better to let the tides nearly cancel out, and to steer as though there were no tide, rather than to keep on the rhumb line by allowing for the tides, steering first to port and then to starboard.

The extra distance which one sails through the water by correcting for the tide can be got from the traverse tables, if one has them. A brief extract which will give you an equally good idea is given under the down-wind sailing section of this chapter. Strangely enough by steering direct the distance travelled *over the ground* is greater. Figure 25 shows the specific

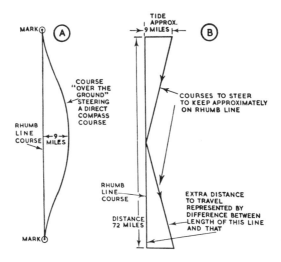

PASSAGE BETWEEN TWO MARKS
ACROSS ONE TIDE (FLOOD & EBB)
ASSUMPTIONS MEAN SPEED OF TIDAL CURRENT 1½ KNOTS
DISTANCE APART OF MARKS 72 MILES
APPROXIMATE YACHTS SPEED 6 KNOTS

Fig. 25

case of a yacht doing about 6 knots on a commanding breeze with 72 miles to go between marks and covering it in just over the 12 hours or one complete tide. Sketch A on the left shows one's path over the ground steering direct allowing oneself to be swept athwart one's direct course and back again. B on the right is a vector diagram showing the courses which one would steer to keep near the rhumb line.

Marks dead to Windward

Circumstances under which it is specially necessary to take account of impending wind changes include those when there is a long turn more or less dead to windward. So at this point we may consider the general strategy of sailing long distances to windward. Supposing one has, as we had in many of the Fastnet Races, 160 miles or so from the Longships to the Fastnet Rock with a nose end breeze and no special incentive in the way of tides, sets, or protected water to encourage one to go one side or other of the 'rhumb line course'. If the wind remains steady one can make the whole distance in two long legs on the port and starboard tacks, or alternatively one can make a succession of comparatively short tacks of say 15 miles a board.

The time taken will be the same in each case, but it is important to note that in general, the latter is much to be preferred. In practice one leg is generally very slightly more favourable than the other and one should plump for this one and go on sailing it until it becomes the unfavourable one by about 5 degrees. For instance suppose that in the seaway in question your experience indicates that your boat will lie within 46 degrees of the wind. The first time you tack, you will be able to check this figure by noting very carefully the mean course for 5 min. before and 5 min. after putting about, and halving the difference between these courses. Plot your D.R. position carefully on the chart, and continue on your tack until your objective (shall we continue to assume it is the 'Fastnet') bears 51 degrees on your weather bow. Then put about, and the Fastnet will if you are correct in your estimate of 46 degrees steered, be 41 degrees on the other bow. Continue again on this new tack, with the Fastnet gradually coming broader on the beam, until on this tack likewise it bears about 51 degrees.

As you get nearer the mark, the boards will get gradually shorter. One is crossing and re-crossing the dead-to-windward line. The reason one should do this in the absence of other factors making it desirable is to be more to one side than the other of the line, is to keep the Fastnet as near as makes no matter dead to windward, so that *any* chance shift of wind is advantageous. These theoretical courses are shown in Fig. 26.

Naturally, as one approaches very near the mark one need not make the number of boards to keep within the 10 degrees arc. But in any event one's last pair of boards should be short ones, to avoid risk of overstanding the mark.

Of course this is the theoretical strategy assuming that the wind is constant. It does not quite work out that way, as there will be minor shifts in

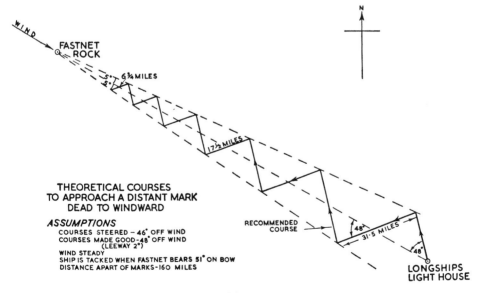

Fig. 26

the wind direction. But this does not alter the fundamental soundness of the thesis which can then be very simply stated. 'In a wind varying in direction choose the leg which points you nearest your mark. Continue sailing this until it becomes definitely the less favourable one by more than 5 degrees. Then it is time to go about.' The word 'definitely' is important since, if one takes account of momentary changes in direction, one will under certain conditions be for ever tacking ship.

But if a shift of wind is forecast one stands more to the side from which the wind is to come. Going out to the Fastnet if the wind is expected to veer one stands more to the northward on the port tack until perhaps the Rock bears Red 61 degrees, then goes about and keeps on to the starboard tack until the Rock bears 51 degrees on the weather bow; then about again on the starboard tack. In this way you will be working always a little to the northward of the windward line. The moment the shift comes, you will be able to bang her round on to the starboard tack; or if you are on it, you may be able to free sheets a shade.

Courses before a Wind Shift

If the shift does not come, no harm is done. But on the other hand it is unwise to stand too far to the north because if the veering shift turns out to be a big one, then one has overstood. Take a look at Fig. 27. Supposing one stands steadily on the port tack until one gets to position X, and the wind then veers 70 degrees, one is no less than 17 miles farther from the

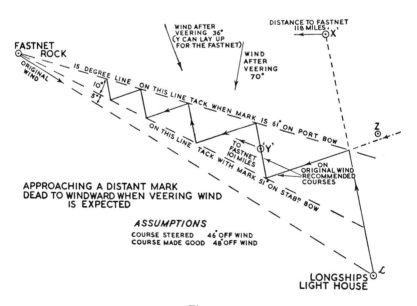

Fig. 27

Fastnet Rock than the man at Y, who has sailed the same distance and both of them have the wind sufficiently free to make approximately their maximum reaching speed. And 17 miles is a matter of at least 2 and maybe 3 hours; it might well decide the race.

One can, if one is prepared to do rather shorter tacks, as a very good alternative, use the 15 degree line only, and make 1-hour boards to the south of it before coming back on to the port tack.

As soon as the wind has veered 36 degrees Y can point up straight for the mark, and as it probably veers gradually farther he will be freed and ahead of X. He has in fact got what northing is really required without over-committing himself. A four-point shift in the wind is very usual in European waters – 'the winds will be moderate, south-westerly to west later in the day' or something of that sort.

This recommendation applies equally when the course between marks is not direct up wind. For instance if one's last mark was at Z, instead of at L, one would enter the tacking areas as shown and proceed as before.

So if you accept this thesis, the rule can be put: 'Turning to windward towards a distant mark in a steady breeze which is expected to veer, keep to the right of the direct windward course but not more than about 15 degrees. If the breeze is expected to back then keep to the left.' The words left and right are used in preference to port and starboard so that there shall be no confusion with the port and starboard tacks which one is making.

A Close Fetch to the Mark

Perhaps the most difficult problem, and also the most fascinating one, is to decide just how free to sail the boat. If the next mark is more or less dead to windward that is one thing; the tactics for these conditions have been discussed, while the technique of getting a boat to windward in a seaway is dealt with in another chapter. For the moment I refer to the situation where it is a close fetch to the mark; which is maybe 50 or 500 miles away. The close-hauled fetch may head you about direct for the mark, or just not enable you to point up for it, and the problem is whether to sail her hard on the wind or a good full – full and bye as the old seamen used to style it – though for them that meant farther off the wind that it does for our modern fore and aft rigs.

If one could assume that the wind was going to remain constant, then the problem is comparatively easy because one sails close-hauled for the mark. But if there is going to be an unpredictable change in wind direction before you get to that mark, which if it is a considerable distance away, is more than likely, then your object is to get as close to the mark as possible by the time that the wind change occurs, regardless of whether that 'distance away' is to leeward related to the present wind.

To illustrate the point (Fig. 28) let us assume that under the conditions in question we can make 5 knots close-hauled and just lay the course, and that by sailing half a point off we can increase our speed to 5·4 knots. If we are clearing the Longships for the Fastnet 160 miles away, and if an appreciable change of wind comes 12 hours later then the difference in position between sailing a straight course and one half a point off is represented by the positions X and Y respectively. If you had sailed a whole point off and made good 5·7 knots, then you would find yourself at Z.

At this time the man who is a whole point off at Z is in the best position, nearest the Fastnet by 6½ miles, though the half-pointer has scored over the direct-liner by 4 miles.

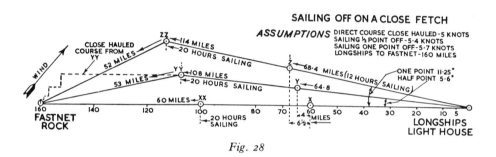

Fig. 28

Now supposing the change of wind comes after 24 hours' steady sailing, then the respective positions would be XX, YY, and ZZ. The half-pointer is nearer the mark by 7 miles, compared to the close-hauled man; if they both sail free to the Fastnet, he will be about an hour ahead. The 'whole-pointer' is just 1 mile nearer the Fastnet still – but at the expense of being very much to the leeward on the original wind.

If no shift in wind direction has come after 24 hours both the 'off course' skippers will be wise to come close-hauled. In fact few people would be prepared to risk carrying on a whole point off so far; they would limit their risk by turning on to the wind earlier, had they sailed that course. They should, however, after coming close-hauled continue on the port tack until it becomes the less favourable by 5 degrees unless there are considerations of current and sheltered water. The straight-liner will of course have done best, but the half-pointer will not have lost much. The whole-pointer is likely to be over 3 hours behind the straight-liner if he comes close-hauled after 24 hours' sailing.

You may say, this is all a gamble on a change of weather – the thing you advised us against. In a way this is true, but between this form of gamble and the general case there is a big difference. In this form you are definitely getting something back, in any case, whether the gamble comes off or not, in the shape of increased speed. It is like backing both ways where your horse can't help being at least placed.

There is one point which though important is not self-evident from the theoretical point of view; that when one decides to sail, say, half a point off and start one's sheets accordingly, one obviates the possibility of pinching due to poor helmsmanship.

The Rule for Close Fetching

The actual case worked out illustrates a truth: 'There is never much risk in sailing half a point off your close-hauled course to gain speed towards a mark at a considerable distance.'

When you come to think of the business of determining your most effective close-hauled course, it is always a matter of opinion and experiment to determine exactly how close it pays to sail. It is clear that one's experience reinforces the graphical conclusion; over a narrow arc of course in the neighbourhood of the optimum, there is not going to be much lost to windward by sailing off a few degrees.

Weighing up the advisability of sailing off wind, one has to bear in mind:
(*a*) The distance of the next mark.
(*b*) The characteristics of the boat under the prevailing conditions.
(*c*) The general steadiness or otherwise of the wind conditions in that area of the world at that time of the year.
(*d*) The particular weather report of the moment.

As regards (*a*) it is obvious that we are only talking of distant marks. Any mark within 25 miles or so must be sailed for close-hauled, and unless there are rather strong indications of impending changes, or unless the conditions are generally variable. So in general must marks up to 40 miles away. In this connection one must bear in mind that should the shift be a slightly heading one, the close-hauled course has paid. Other things being the same the more distant the mark the more worth while is the gamble.

Concerning (*b*) it is generally the heavier cruising type which will gain most by being sailed off – boats of the Beta division under English rules.

The *actual* gain in speed by 'sailing off' a normal cruiser is possibly about the same as that in most modern ocean racers, but the gain *relative to the close-hauled speed* is greater.

Close Fetching with various Rigs

But more modern boats may score heavily under certain special circumstances. In a modern yawl rig, with a good gap between the mainsail leech and mizzen mast, if you were prepared to sail about a point and a quarter (about 14 degrees) off, you could set a mizzen staysail, increasing your total sail area by about 18 per cent. This would be very valuable in light weather.

It is largely a question of knowing your boat and how she will react to sailing off under the various wind and sea conditions, and it is important that one should take every opportunity of gaining data. If you have a speed variation indicator this will make things easier. If not, one can resort to half-hourly log readings, being careful regarding the time of reading, since a minute each side of the half-hour will give you a 2 in 30 or a 6·7 per cent error. Or in light weather one can use the Dutchman's log: a piece of wood or some object unaffected by the wind is dropped clear of the ship forward and timed between the stem and as it passes the counter end, with a stop-watch. Quite accurate results are obtained at speeds which are too low to be properly recorded by patent log. For convenience, I make out a table for the speeds 'for every second' so that the speed can be read off directly the time has been taken.

As an instance of the necessity for knowing one's boat's performance – lest one takes quite a wrong decision concerning the amount of 'sail off' – *Myth* sailing in light winds is an interesting example. In Force 1 her fastest point of sailing is five points off the wind. There is therefore no point, in this weather, in ramping her off.

Bermuda Race Conditions compared to Hobart Race

As regards item (*d*), concerning the general weather conditions for the time of the year, we may usefully compare the two big races in which there are long straight legs. The Bermuda Race is a direct course the whole of the 635 miles. The Sydney–Hobart, of 650 miles, has 570 miles or so in the same general direction with only minor alterations in courses to exploit the current. But the latter race has three sets of wind conditions in that distance; the first down the coast of New South Wales, the second across the Bass Straits, and then the south-eastern coast of Tasmania.

It is pretty clear that in the Hobart race we can generally count on a real wind shift a couple of times during the passage. But experience indicates that 65 to 70 per cent of the races will be sailed with the wind free and of this spinnakers will be set perhaps 35 per cent of the time.

In the Bermuda Race the crossing of the Gulf Stream (which often occupies a band some 120 miles wide towards the end of the first half of the race), generally results in fireworks of some sort or another, be it only a few mild squalls. But this does not alter the fact that most of the wind comes from the same school, and as often as not if you start on the starboard leg you sail most of the race on this tack. Therefore it will be by no means safe to bet on a fundamental wind change in the course of the race.

Fastnet Conditions

It is rare for the Fastnet Race to be sailed without some major wind change occurring in the course of the race. But then there is no leg as long as the others in question and it is often possible for the passage from the Scillies to the Fastnet to be made without a major shift. Similarly for the return trip; one cannot definitely count on a shift in that time. On the other hand one is somewhat more likely to have a wind change of some sort on the first long portion of the course, that is to say between clearing the Isle of Wight and arriving off the Lizard.

Our fourth factor (*d*) 'The particular weather report of the moment' needs no elaboration in the present connection.

Rough Rule for Sailing Off

If you decide to go in for a bit of 'sailing off', you will find the following additional general rule useful, particularly when conditions do not enable you to sit down to very extensive or accurate plotting: 'On a close fetch if you sail off a whole point to leeward, from close-hauled, to gain speed, and no shift of wind arrives or is in early prospect by the time you have sailed half the distance to your mark, you should then come close-hauled again. But if you have sailed off only half a point you can wait for your shift till you have sailed two-thirds of the distance.'

Figure 29 gives you an idea of the extra distance you have to cover owing to various deviations from the direct course, resulting perhaps from a decision to sail fuller or more to windward; or perhaps to go looking for wind or for set, or for some other reason.

The direct distance between the two marks is assumed to be 100 miles.

DISTANCES COVERED BETWEEN TWO MARKS
ONE HUNDRED MILES APART DUE TO
DEVIATIONS FROM A DIRECT COURSE

INITIAL DEVIATION MADE FROM THE DIRECT COURSE	PROPORTION OF DISTANCE COVERED BEFORE RESUMING THE DIRECT COURSE			
	A 1/5	B 2/5	C 3/5	D 4/5
5°	100·05	100·2	100·45	100·7
10°	100·53	101·0	102·4	105·8
15°	101·0	102·3	105·1	111·7
20°	101·7	104·3	109·3	120·0
25°	102·6	106·9	115·0	130·4
30°	104·6	110·3	121·8	143·0

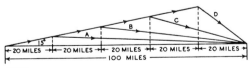

NOTE:
IT WILL BE POSSIBLE TO INTERPOLATE FOR INTERMEDIATE
COURSES AND FOR TURNS MADE AT OTHER POINTS. AS THE
BASE DISTANCE IS 100, THE INCREASES IN DISTANCE CAN
BE TREATED AS PERCENTAGES AND EASILY APPLIED TO OTHER
BASE DISTANCES.

Fig. 29

The actual distances covered shown in column A assume that one resumes the direct course after covering one-fifth of the distance; column B after two-fifths of the distance; C, three-fifths; and D, four-fifths. The explanatory sketch represents graphically the four different alternative courses, A, B, C, D, for a 15 degree initial deviation.

Tactics for Reaching

If the mark is at some distance it is very often permissible to make a slight deviation from the direct course in order to get a particular sail to draw. As already mentioned half a point off may well enable you to get the mizzen staysail set; and in light weather this may pay handsomely. For instance in *Orion*, the bigger mizzen staysail was 600 sq. ft. Similarly a slight alteration of course, perhaps to leeward, or maybe to windward, might well enable a particularly favourable combination of sails to draw between the masts of a schooner.

In light going and a beam wind, even with a sloop or cutter, it may well pay you to sail half the way to your mark with a genoa set, pointing say a point high of your mark (and travelling faster than with the wind just about the beam), and at half-way if the wind were still in the same direction, to turn on to a direct course for the mark which will then bring the wind a point abaft the beam, and set a spinnaker, so that it can really pull effectively. In connection with such deviations, Figure 29 will be of interest.

The possibility of exploiting such advantages will depend on the particular rig and outfit of sails in your boat. But in any case they are light weather tactics: in fresher conditions it will normally pay to go straight for your mark.

The Weather Mark – Holding to Windward

There is another quite separate aspect of reaching, which applies only to approaching a fairly near mark, or obstruction to sea room – which is the question how much windwarding should be kept in hand. Allowance is normally made only for minor variation in wind direction and only for a small amount of 'heading' by the wind. When the wind is on or abaft the beam, no allowance need be made, since a minor change still leaves the wind free. With the wind $4\frac{1}{2}$ to $5\frac{1}{2}$ points on the bow, however, a heading of 1 or 2 points will result in being unable to lay the mark. Therefore it is customary to lay up for a while a little above the mark, perhaps half a point, if it can be done without too much sacrifice of speed – this will depend on the boat and on the sea conditions. I say 'for a while' because when one has slowly worked to a safe distance to windward – and it should be slowly to avoid an undue deviation from the correct course – one resumes a direct course.

The exact action to be taken varies so much on circumstances that it is difficult to be more specific than this. The amount one works up may be increased if the mark is not in sight, perhaps owing to fog or weather, if one is uncertain of one's position, always provided there is no risk of sailing right past the mark. In the case of the Fastnet for instance there is no such risk, since the coast behind will come up. But if the mark is a lightship well off shore, then one can't afford to work to weather to an extent which will unduly increase the chance of missing it altogether.

It should be noted that this refers to marks which are being approached from, say, under 30 miles. When being approached from a considerable distance the chances of a change of weather make the speed aspect more important than that of the exact course for the mark.

Tactics in Down Wind Sailing

Let us first consider the conditions when the wind is dead aft or fine on the quarter. The one rule we must get firmly in our minds from the start is this: 'never run by the lee'. You may say that this is obvious. But just the same, once the main boom is nicely guyed forward, one is apt to find the helmsman hanging on to the course ordered, carefully watching his compass; while he has failed to realise that the wind has crept round to his lee quarter.

In light or moderate weather running by the lee results in a serious loss of speed. In strong winds the effect is less serious, but one will not be tempted to do this on account of the discomfort and risk of gybing.

So as soon as there is any tendency to run by the lee, she should be quietly luffed to bring the wind fine on the proper quarter. This may take you out of your course, but the loss will be less than running by the lee. Should the change in the wind hold, one can eventually gybe. But while you are preparing to gybe, rigging fresh guys and so on, you should be luffed out and not running by the lee.

The apparent wind when astern is more changeable than when ahead, as we see in Fig. 30, and so one has to be continually on the look-out, and in light weather be prepared to steer a comparatively zigzag course in order to keep the wind slightly on the quarter.

As we can see again from Fig. 30, the apparent wind is always more out on the quarter (farther ahead) than the true wind. This means that after gybing one has only to bring the true wind slightly on the new weather quarter for the sails to fill properly. The importance of this is in connection with the question of how soon to gybe. Tacking down wind will be dealt with separately, but the point I want to make at the moment is that only a relatively small change of course will bring the apparent wind from nicely out on one quarter to nicely out on the other. Therefore in moderate winds, where the question of sailing well up into the wind to increase speed does not arise, a gybe can profitably be made rather earlier than might be expected. This is not easy to understand, but it is worth a little study and thought.

In light winds one travels appreciably faster with the wind nicely out on

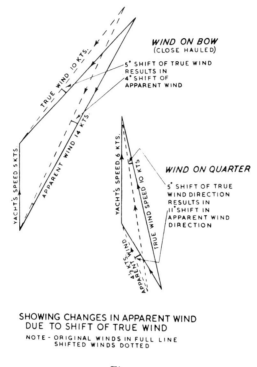

SHOWING CHANGES IN APPARENT WIND
DUE TO SHIFT OF TRUE WIND
NOTE - ORIGINAL WINDS IN FULL LINE
SHIFTED WINDS DOTTED

Fig. 30

the quarter, rather than with the wind fine on the quarter, because one's apparent wind speed is increased. The problem, and it is not any easy one to solve, is how much running up towards the wind pays?

Sailing Up to Light Breezes

The first thing to note is that unlike the problem of a close fetch, where we were also estimating how much off the direct track to sail to gain speed, the sideways deflection off the rhumb line course is not as a rule of any importance. Either the mark is so far away that the deflection is geometrically negligible, or if the mark is nearer, one can run into the rhumb line on the other gybe under the same conditions as one ran out. Gybing under light conditions is a comparatively easy business and should waste very little time; of course, without lowering the spinnaker.

Tacking Down Wind

If, as one can, one assumes that the deflection is to be neglected, then the ratio of the distance travelled when sailing off course to the direct distance is the secant of the angle between the courses. The extra distance to be covered expressed as a percentage for various courses, that is to say for various amounts of sailing off (down wind) course is as follows:

5 degrees – 0·4 per cent
10 degrees – 1·5 per cent
15 degrees – 3·5 per cent
20 degrees – 6·4 per cent
25 degrees – 10·3 per cent
30 degrees – 15·5 per cent
35 degrees – 22·1 per cent
40 degrees – 30·5 per cent

This table explains more quickly and definitely than any other way, why tacking down wind can pay. It is clear that the gain in speed necessary to make 20 degrees deviation is easily attained.

It pays to steer 20 degrees up if one's speed increases by more than one-sixteenth. If you are in light wind doing 3 knots this is one-fifth of a knot; and the actual gain might well be half a knot.

So difficult is it to get any practical speed figures, that it is better in very light winds to sail two points up and leave it at that. But this is only in light winds. At other times the sailing up should be confined to the amount necessary to ensure that the wind is just on the quarter rather than dead astern.

In fact the spinnaker set in light airs the apparent wind is so variable that it is often best to sail so as to keep the *apparent* wind about 40 degrees out on the quarter and accept whatever course this gives one – a pretty zigzag one, but possibly the best speed you can get; and it may obviate the need for constant sail trimming and disturbing the spinnaker. A good deal will depend on the direction of the sea which may affect the steadiness or otherwise of the boat, and in turn the amount of wind one can hold in a spinnaker, which one is striving to keep full and drawing, in a tumble of sea.

With two-masted rigs the necessity for sailing up is often greater than with cutters or sloops, so as to put the 'tween-mast light sails to work. This is particularly so in the case of the schooner with the big light fisherman sail; this will be comparable in size with the spinnaker which can only be set from the foremast head in a schooner, under normal racing rules.

In the case of yawls and ketches if a $2\frac{1}{2}$ point alteration in course, to bring the wind from near astern to well out on the quarter, enables the mizzen staysail to be got to draw – then in very light winds this will probably pay. It won't do any worth-while work with the breeze right aft.

But finally one must make the point that this sailing up can only really pay when you have the proper full-allowed size of spinnakers, of modern cut, and in the case of two-masted ships, light 'tween-mast sails of maximum area.

Tailpiece

Warp Knitted Sails

Jeremy Howard-Williams

With one exception, the tailpieces are magazine articles originally published as spoofs to satirize the sailing world gently and try to hoodwink the unwary reader. Jeremy Howard-Williams writes of this one:

'*I was inspired to write* Warp Knitted Sails *by hearing a serious radio broadcast on development in the textile industry. Remembering Owen Torrey's brilliant piece on* The Black Deck, *I strove not to emulate but to follow.*

'*The article was first published in* Yachts and Yachting *and was the cause of a letter from a reader. A designer in the "shrinking double jersey industry" wrote to tell me that "double jersey is weft knitted and not warp knitted as stated (the machines knit from weft to wight) and is of no use to the sailmaker. Give us details" he said.*

'*Not to be lured into giving away secrets, I was cagey in my reply (I had run out of inspiration). The influence of the weft is radical, I said, and followed it with as much technical jargon as could be got into a couple of lines. "If my correspondent thinks I am naïve enough to reveal anything more than the most elementary data, he must have a warped sense of humour."*

'*There was also a serious enquiry from ICI, no less. I hope readers of this book won't ask any more awkward questions, because I don't know the answers – honestly.*'

So you think that a sail made from a single piece of material, without seams or any darts for shaping, is pure fantasy? Not so; computer-controlled machines capable of fashioning sails in one piece to the minutest measurement and degree of flow are already in existence. Tomorrow's sails are being tested today.

It is now twenty-six years since the first commercial Terylene sail in Britain was made by Gowens – a genoa for 'Sonda' in 1952. This was the concrete evidence of a major technological leap forward in materials as the scientist moved into the sailing scene. Since then progress has been rapid, to the point where weaving of sailcloth has nearly reached the limit of refinement. So the scientist has been turning his attention to the way in which the fabric is produced – process development.

Quietly, in the secluded confines of the laboratory, a revolution in textile technology has been taking place. The vast resources of the industry have been harnessed to investigate the whole concept of cloth production, going back to basic principles, with an eye on the mass market in all forms of materials. Quick to grasp the spin-off sailcloth producers have evolved their own programmes.

The inefficient to-and-fro action of the shuttle, involving acceleration, deceleration, stopping and reverse movement, was an obvious target and, after considerable experiment, one of the older forms of cloth manufacture was critically re-assessed.

Knitting proved highly susceptible to modernisation and has moved from the hearth to the automated factory.

Double jersey fabric, suitably treated, has become an important part of the textile industry generally and sailmaking in particular, construction being programmed by computer, and the cloth building up on a circular drum which rotates smoothly without the constant interruption of a reciprocating shuttle, in a process called warp-knitting. Parallel with this development, cloth is being produced by punching needles into a mat of fibres, while a third non-woven process involves laying synthetic fibres on a moving belt until the fabric is built up in a cohesive whole.

Of these lines of development, warp-knitting has proved to be the best suited to sailcloth. Using the advantages of modern techniques, complete sails can be constructed of one homogeneous cloth to any desired shape, without recourse to artificial seams, patches or tedious shaping stratagems. The sail is built up in a three-dimensional process which is controlled by a computer (so exact, that instant repetition is easy) by what is known to the trade as engineered tailoring. Warp-knitting works without needles, with very few moving parts, and it is particularly suitable for producing cloth of all weights, using a variety of fibres.

The owners of traditional gaff cutters, only recently reconciled to talking in terms of polyester, heat sealing and modulus of extensibility, will now have to grapple with a new vocabulary which includes sliver knitting,

crossfolded wadding, two-bowl crabbing, backlaying, billowing and scour-
ing by means of ballooning off the winch.

The world's leading sailmakers have been watching these developments
with some interest. Determined to be in the forefront, Ratseys have been
frantically costing the mammoth task of being first to replace their present
looms with warp-knitting rotary machines, while Ted Hood claims to have
already produced the first fully-fashioned seamless knitted sail for secret
trials, far from prying eyes, north of the ice line in Canadian waters.
Rumour has it that North Sailmakers reckon to be a jump ahead through
adapting the punched mat technique in a novel tri-needle form (a suit of
sails will cost more than the boat, but it will save money in the end), and
strange stories are circulating in the City and Wall Street that Bruce Banks
has obtained a controlling interest in ICI Fibres.

One advantage of warp-knitting is that, by careful tension control, a
sailcloth can be produced which does away with the need for reefing. As
windspeed increases, the material stretches and air is allowed to penetrate
the cloth, thus progressively reducing pressure on the fabric. Professor C
A Marchaj, fresh from writing an even more complicated book than his
formidable *Sailing Theory and Practice,* has spent hundreds of hours in the
wind tunnel at the Department of Aeronautics and Astronautics of
Southampton University and run up a pretty hefty phone bill talking to his
opposite number at the Massachusetts Institute of Technology. He has
been heard muttering about osmotic bleed of air from the high pressure
side of an aerofoil to produce what he calls servo-controlled vacuum lift.
He considers servo mechanism to be important because close control is
vital, and must be monitored by automatic pressure valves incorporated in
the clew and tack fittings. Rumours that the exorbitant cost of this
development could only be met by the Government caused a rush of
potential America's Cup challengers, eager not to be denied their right to
empty their pockets and what is more, Marchaj has infuriated these 12
Metre owners because he has refused to use either waste uranium or gold,
preferring to stay a jump ahead of the rule makers, because he plans that
the valves shall be made of pig-iron, thus avoiding any danger of an exotic
material penalty. The concomitant bulk of the equipment will be offset by
casings which themselves will act as turbulence generators, contributing
still further to lift. The professor reckons that every sailplan since the days
of the square rig will be outdated at the stroke of a pen. The backs of
crumpled envelopes salvaged from his waste paper basket reveal that the
great man's mind has also been working on the antidote: lift generated by
rolling cylinders' trailing tip vortices in a viscous fluid. As he has been
heard to mutter on more than one occasion, 'If we have

$$\frac{L}{b} = V_o \beta,$$

then it is obvious that we can write

$$L = \rho V_o (V_c^2 \pi r_o) \times b'$$

Meanwhile the sailmakers have been scrambling to recruit little old ladies from the crofts of the Shetland Isles and the backwoods of Kentucky. The more astute of these craftswomen are reported to be earning vast fortunes as technical advisers on such complex problems as turning the heel at the tack of a full mainsail, or grafting at the shoulders of a spinnaker. Some of the smaller sailmakers are short-circuiting the warp-knitting process by employing these experts as direct labour to produce sails on ultra-long needles to pirated designs. Cases have already occurred where the patent honesty of the ladies in question has thrown the activities of headhunting firms and industrial spies into confusion. Used to the rather more devious attitudes adopted as normal by the business world, organisations trying to recruit experienced knitters have retired baffled by their innocence and battered by their rolled umbrellas. Business management seminars now include at least one session on the problems of honesty, and how to cope with a cup of tea, a buttered tea-cake and a penetrating simplicity if the best sailmakers are to be acquired.

Star-crossed

This picture was taken by Flip Schulke at the 1969 Bacardi Cup in Miami, Florida. The incident took place at the start of one of the races. The participants were, from the left, 4041, a boat from Maryland, 4100, Dr Jaretski from New York and 4637, Bert Williams from Chicago. The boat on the right was to weather of 4041, and took her wind, causing the leeward boat to come upright suddenly. Their masthead halyard tubes and halyards fouled each other. 4100 was behind, coming through, and by the time he saw the masts hooked he was committed. One second after this picture, his mast hit the other two and broke them apart. He sailed the race, but the other two had to retire. Neither mast broke, but both were ruined by compression cracks. The photographer was well placed to take this picture at the time, for he was taking pictures for the Race Committee. I am indebted for this information to Flip Schulke and to Frank Zagarino of the Star Class Association.

Racing: Then and Now

Cutter Yachts

John Leather
Gaff Rig
first published 1970

This section includes four pieces on offshore racing which chart its development over the last 200 years. The first one, from John Leather's Gaff Rig, *tells of the cutter yachts which dominated yacht racing for the first 150 years. The author writes:*

'*When I was writing* Gaff Rig *I particularly wished to include something expressing my admiration for the captains, crews, designers and builders of the large racing yachts before 1939. These great cutters, schooners and yawls gradually reached near-perfection in efficiency of the gaff rig by the 1920s and their conception, construction and handling combined the skills of many men.*

'*The captains and crews on many of them came from my own Rowhedge: a small village on the river Colne in Essex, on the east coast of England, where a population of 1000 was almost wholly maritime until 1939 and prolonged its skills in shipbuilding long after. Many relatives for generations raced in these large yachts, the handling of which was their pride and art, as it was of their contemporaries from nearby Brightlingsea, Wivenhoe, Tollesbury and West Mersea who, with others from the Solent, the Clyde and later from the West Country, manned the British racing fleet. Two of these relatives captained three challengers for the America's Cup; others were mates and mastheadmen, bowspritendsmen and hands. Their fore and aft seamanship had matured quickly in the winter fisheries, under sail in the village's fleet of cutter- and ketch-rigged smacks. Their traditions remained strong and were passed on to others like myself: mid-twentieth-century youngsters sailing our small boats. I have recorded much of their lore and achievements in my book* The Northseamen.

'*Some of their attitudes to the sea are enduringly desirable. One thinks particularly of their quiet competence under all conditions and unassuming self-reliant approach to seafaring in small sailing craft, the ability to work swiftly and with strength in weather from calm to gale, the constant attention to hull, rig and maintenance of a yacht in excellent condition.*

'*So, much of the chapter* Cutter Yachts *is a salute to the traditions of mentors and old friends whose knowledge of gaff rig will never be surpassed, but whose racing instincts naturally accepted the greater windward efficiency of the bermudian rig as soon as it appeared.*'

The cutter rig was, and still is, widely used in England, Europe and Scandinavia for yachts of all sizes. Sloop rig and the boomless gaff sail were common in pleasure craft until the late-18th century when cutters were developing rapidly. A yacht club was formed at Starcross, Devon, in 1773 and in 1776 Cowes held its first regatta, sailed by working craft. Southampton followed, and in 1783 a race for Essex fishing cutters was held in the Blackwater and was won by a Burnham smack. A few months later cutters from Rowhedge, Wivenhoe, Brightlingsea and Mersea raced for a silver cup and suit of colours. These events survive in the annual regattas of those places, where smacks still race. Similar racing spread along the east and south coasts.

In all these events yachts were present as a minority of onlookers and few existed before 1800, when there were probably not more than 70 in England, mostly cutter rigged. Such craft were generally built without thought of racing and to no arbitrary limits of size or rig. Most owners required comfortable craft of imposing appearance with ample accommodation for cruising coastwise and to the Continent and Baltic. Their crews were largely drawn from the Colne, Thames and Solent seamen sailing similar smacks and other small craft.

After about 1780, yacht designing and building began to emerge as a distinct branch of naval architecture and craft were built for pleasure sailing and racing. Many were small, but some surprisingly large for these troubled times at sea. At first there was great similarity between the largest and fastest of these yachts and contemporary government fishing, and smuggling cutters. Gradually yachts began to emerge as a type and speed became increasingly important as racing became fashionable after 1800, often between pairs of yachts for high wagers, and many fine cutters were built in Essex, Sussex, Hampshire and the Isle of Wight.

Notable among them was Philip Sainty's most famous creation, the large cutter yacht *Pearl*; built at Colchester in 1819 for the Marquis of Anglesey, a veteran of Waterloo and confidant of kings and statesmen. Before 1809 Sainty had built, at his Colchester yard, the very fast cutter yacht *Emerald* for the Marquis who, home from the wars, wanted a giant cutter which was to be the fastest in the country. He found Sainty in gaol for smuggling, together with his son and brother Robert, but got them all out by influence, to build the new yacht which Philip designed with characteristic skill, as displayed by her recorded lines. *Pearl* was 113 registered tons, making her a giant among contemporary yachts which averaged between 20 and 70 tons. She displaced 127·5 tons on dimensions of 65 ft 4 in lwl × 19 ft 6 in × 11 ft 6 in draft. Her form was beautifully easy and fair and in an era of bluff bows she was notable for a fine entrance blending almost imperceptibly into a long run terminating in a delicately proportioned counter.

In contrast to her hull the vast cutter rig would excite little comment from seamen seeking their winter living in fishing smacks and smugglers so rigged. *Pearl's* flax canvas totalled 3,218 square feet in the loose-footed mainsail, staysail and jib, but excluding the gaff topsail. Off the wind she set a square topsail, spread by a barren-yard below it, which was, typically, lowered to the bulwarks when not in use. For racing she set a long-yarded gaff topsail and added studding sails to the topsail leech and a ringtail to the mainsail. In light weather the sail luffs were drenched with water to hold a better wind; some yachts being specially fitted with pumps and hoses to aid in skeating, as this practice was called. *Pearl* surpassed all expectations on trials and the Marquis settled £100 a year on Sainty on condition that he did not build a yacht for anyone else, but he broke the contract and quickly resumed shipbuilding at Wivenhoe, continuing to specialise in fast craft

Cutter racing rapidly became popular but there was no time allowance then for differences in size. In 1825 the 85 ton Lymington built *Arrow*, designed three years previously by her owner, Joseph Weld, challenged *Pearl* to race from Cowes to Swanage and return for £500. The Marquis was so certain of victory that, in accepting, he vowed 'If the *Pearl* should be beaten I will burn her as soon as we get back.' He must have regretted his words early in the race when *Arrow* led, but *Pearl* eventually won by 10½ minutes and escaped a fiery end.

By then owners had discovered that a good large yacht could beat a good small one and a number of large yachts were built on the south coast to beat the Essex flier, whose bow they copied. In 1826 *Pearl* and *Arrow* met their match racing the 103 ton *Nautilus*, built by Lynn Ratsey of Cowes, which completely outsailed them for a prize of £500, although never again did *Nautilus* distinguish herself for they 'fished her mast and killed her', as the old sailors said.

Instead of the flying start we use today, these early races started with the yachts anchored or moored to starting buoys, about a cable apart, usually with all sails lowered, but sometimes with only headsails down. At the second gun all canvas was hoisted and anchors or springs rattled home in a frenzy of activity.

Cutter racing fever gripped yacht owners and sail areas increased alarmingly, accentuated by the 1826 ban on extra sails, which led to ordinary rig of immense size and consequently larger hulls to carry it. Ballast was increased and a proportion of it was shifted to windward when racing; a practice frowned on by many. All these early races were sailed by professional crews, hailing mainly from the Colne and Solent areas, and great was their rivalry. They took racing seriously and there were incidents such as the fouling of *Arrow* by *Miranda*, when the crews set about each other with windlass handspikes and axes.

In this atmosphere the peak of early rivalry dawned in 1823 with the launch of the south coast cutters *Lulworth*, 127 tons, for Joseph Weld, and the 162 ton *Louisa* for Lord Belfast. During the next two years interest focused on the tussles between them and the *Meani*; all being stripped out for racing. The rivalry of Belfast and Weld culminated in 1830 with the building of Wild's giant cutter *Alarm,* queen of the south coast and the terror of racing men for generations. This 193-tonner was one of the largest cutters ever built. To match her Philip Sainty's Wivenhoe yard launched *Arundel,* 188 ton cutter for the Duke of Norfolk, a yacht contemporarily described as 'the finest sea-going cutter ever built', and occasionally she out-sailed both *Alarm* and *Louisa,* but inside the Wight the giant *Alarm* was supreme. Competition and experiment was rife and began a craze for lengthening and rebuilding the cutters as they became outclassed by new yachts, and *Arrow* was continually rebuilt and still winning prizes into the 1870s, and was not broken up until 1903.

After a decade of hotly contested racing these big cutters had their day in 1834, when many races were restricted to craft under 75 tons and the most colourful period of yacht racing's early days was closed. Racing and development of cutter yachts lagged for several years while various attempts were made to introduce fair competition by using tonnage rules measuring length on the keel and breadth, but ignoring depth and sail area. Although schooners and even brigs occasionally raced, the cutter rig was recognised as so superior in weatherliness that it was naturally selected for most yachts built for racing.

Several early racing cutters were built of iron, but it did not become popular as the bottoms could not be kept smooth. In 1844 the iron cutters *Bluebell*, *Belvedire* and *Ariel* from the Thames raced at Cowes but were beaten by a wooden cutter owned and built by the brothers T and J Wanhill of Poole, Dorset, who became noted yachtbuilders. In 1845 the big cutters received a rude shock when the little 35 ton cutter *Heroine,* built by Wanhills to the design of Thomas Musslewhite, their draughtsman, and sailed by John Nicholls of Southampton, beat *Alarm* which had been the champion racing yacht of England for years. The Wanhills' cutters were much finer shaped than any then built and instituted rule cheating by raking the sternpost to reduce keel length, decreasing the beam and increasing the depth, besides having considerable internal ballast to maintain power to carry a large sail area, without increasing tonnage. Unfortunately, many desirable qualities were sacrificed to gain speed. They were uncomfortably wet boats, pitching heavily with lean bows and heavy ballast, and needed a big crew to handle the large sail plans, besides having little space for accommodation.

Wanhills' cutters were often winners, particularly *Phantom* and *Vision,* but fast craft were also being designed and built by Thomas Harvey of Wivenhoe, Essex. In 1832 he had bought Philip Sainty's shipyard and continued its tradition of building fast yachts, fishing and merchant vessels. In 1845 Harvey launched the cutter *Prima Donna* which quickly became top of the flourishing 25 ton class. His next big success was the 40-tonner *Amazon*, built at his other shipyard at Ipswich, Suffolk in 1851, and closely followed by the 48 ton cutter *Volante* which, sailed by Captain James Pittuck of Wivenhoe, had a tremendous success and was lying second to the schooner *America* in the historic 1851 race round the Isle of Wight, *Volante* having sailed the correct course, when she broke her bowsprit and gave up. Had the spar held, yachting history could have been radically different.

Thomas Harvey's son John was apprenticed to his father and showed great promise as a designer of very fast craft. When very young he designed and superintended the building of the 40 ton racing cutter *Avalon* in 1850 and next year was running the Wivenhoe Shipyard which during the following thirty years became famous for fast yachts of all sizes besides scores of smacks, and schooners for the fruit trades. In 1852 John Harvey designed and built the noted 10 tonner *Kitten* with very advanced hull shape; her profile being daringly cut away to reduce wetted surface, similarly to that later regarded as revolutionary in the large yacht *Jullanar* of 1875 whose design was actually carried out by John Harvey, though the credit is usually ascribed solely to her owner.

John Harvey evolved and draughted his designs from mathematical principles and was later a founder member of the Royal Institute of Naval Architects. He was famous for his cutters and the best included *Thought*, *Syren*, *Dione*, *Audax*, *Snowdrop*, *Resolute* and *Dagmar*, owned by the Prince of Wales, later King Edward VII.

In 1865 John Harvey had the curious experience of acting as joint umpire with Dan Hatcher, for a series of Solent races between the cutters *Thought*, designed by Harvey in 1852 and the iron-hulled *Torpid*, the winner to become owner of both yachts and a £200 stake. *Torpid*, which carried seven racing captains among her crew of twenty, won, and both cutters were towed triumphantly up Southampton Water by their victorious owner's steam yacht.

By the 1840s the traditional pattern of British yacht racing evolved; the season commencing on the Thames at the end of May and continuing until the end of August at scores of important regattas from Harwich, round the coast to the Clyde and including Ireland, the west and south coasts and the West Country, the racing yachts sailing several thousand miles during the summer.

Shifting ballast was banned in 1856 but during the 19th century 'the Cutter' became synonymous with a narrow, deep draught, plumb-bowed yacht having a counter stern, oversparred and over-canvassed for hard weather, wet in a seaway but able to beat to windward through almost anything, provided she was properly reefed and the crew could stand it and stay aboard. This exaggerated type of cutter yacht resulted from the Thames Measurement tonnage rating rule which was introduced in 1854 and remained in force until 1878. This taxed beam twice but allowed unrestricted draught, forcing English designers to reduce beam and achieve stability by ballasting, at first all inside but later with increasing amount hung on the keel. Length was measured from the stem to the sternpost, on deck, resulting in plumb bows and long counters and, as sail area was disregarded altogether, the powerful and versatile cutter rig flourished and attained excessive area. The legend of this exaggerated type of cutter yacht has persisted and is often, wrongly, regarded as the only true breed. Outclassed racing yachts became useful cruisers with sail plans reduced, and sometimes made seaworthy pilot and fishing craft.

However, the contrast with working cutters, often designed and built alongside cutter yachts, is interesting as in them builders retained to the end the healthy beam and proportions which were denied the racers.

Robert Aldous of Brightlingsea, Essex, built many fast cutters of both types and became noted for the windward ability of his 9 ton racer *Violet* built in 1855. In 1858 Aldous built another *Violet* which, renamed *Christabel*, became the most famous of his yachts. Like many cutters of the time she was lengthened three years after launch and emerged as a fast boat, winning races all round the coast and the 'ocean' race from Cherbourg to Ryde. In 1866 she was again sawn in two and lengthened to come storming into Harwich winning the Down Swin race. In the boisterous Nore to Dover she led seventeen big cutters and schooners, and the enormous 209 ton open lugger yacht *New Moon*, only to be just beaten by the big schooner *Egeria* within yards of Dover Harbour where 10,000 spectators cheered her gallant effort.

Until 1866 Aldous rivalled the five other noted yacht builders of that period: Harvey of Wivenhoe, Wanhill brothers of Poole, Dan Hatcher of Southampton, Inman of Lymington and William Fife II of Fairlie. Until 1880 Dan Hatcher, followed by his son, built many fast cutters up to the 40 ton class, his early success being the *Gleam* of 1855. Most were designed by William Shergold, Hatcher's draughtsman, and were of composite construction, with beautiful lines.

When running, early racing cutters set a square-sail with a triangular raffee topsail above. In 1865 Hatcher built the cutter *Niobe* for William Gordon whose skipper was Captain Thomas Diaper (sen) of Itchen. Between them they devised a triangular running sail to be set from the masthead, with its clew boomed out in the manner which headsails had been boomed out for years before, except in racers where their sheet had to be held by hand. Having tried it outside the Needles *Niobe* first set it racing on the Thames against the iron cutter *Vindex*, beating her by its efficiency when running. The sail became known as the *niobe* and was known in the racing fleet by this name for four or five years until the yacht clubs wanted a different name for it, when for no explicable reason, despite its later use in the yacht *Sphinx*, it was called a spinnaker, and has remained so since.

After 1865 the south of England yachts had increasingly to reckon with competitors from Clyde builders. The first William Fife was a Scottish wheelwright who built rowing boats in his spare time at Fairlie, Ayrshire, on the Firth of Clyde. His boatbuilding prospered and eclipsed his wheelwright trade. He established a yard which built small commercial craft and yachts, principally cutters. Fairlie was a most unpromising site for what became a noted yachtyard. For many years yachts were built in the open on the rocky shallow foreshore which made launching of anything but small craft very difficult, and the anchorage was exposed.

Fife's son William (II) joined the business bringing a flair for design. The 55 ft cutter *Cymba*, launched from the yard in 1852, won many prizes but young Fife's masterpiece was *Fiona* of 1865, the most noted cutter of her day when sailed by Captain John Houston of Largs, with a crew of local yacht hands who, surprisingly, turned to weaving rather than seafaring for a winter living. For a time *Fiona* turned the tide of south county racing cutters' success. She was a noted early design of Fife II with dimensions of 75 ft 7 in × 15 ft 8 in × 11 ft 10 in draught.

Houston was a determined racing skipper. Once hard pressed in a breeze by the cutter *Vanguard* sailed by Captain Harry Thompson of Itchen, both yachts were carrying their huge spinnakers too long, running for the finish when they would gybe over the line. To save time Houston ordered *Fiona*'s spinnaker to be cut away and with a thunderclap it blew clear as she gybed and won. John Houston carried sail excessively and frequently broke spars but his determination, and *Fiona*'s weatherliness, established Fife's name in the racing world. The Fifes' next great success came in a roundabout way; in 1872 Boag, also of Fairlie, built the 36 ft cutter *Cloud* for the 10 ton class, and a lanky young Essexman named Lemon Cranfield, from Rowhedge, was appointed captain. He raced her with such success that two years later he was selected to race the 62 ton *Neva* just launched by Fife to challenge the big class. Lemon brought a crew of fellow villagers with him and made her name a legend for speed. At Rothesay in 1876 *Neva* raced *Cuckoo*, sailed by Jack Wyatt of Hythe, with a Hampshire crew, and beat her by one second. Lemon used his wonderful judgment in tacking to fetch the mark exactly, within a foot. During 1877 he won £1,335 in prize money and became the acknowledged genius of yacht racing in which no man, before or since, has had such spectacular success. His five younger brothers were also top racing captains.

Restriction of beam and practical ballasting considerations caused British designers to achieve stiffness by maintaining a relatively low sail plan, long in the base. Booms still extended well outboard and bowsprits were very long. Figure 31 is the typical sail plan of the large class racing cutter *Vanduara* built of steel by D & W Henderson of Glasgow in 1880, to designs by young George Watson, who had hitherto only designed small yachts.

The arrangement and proportions of her rig typify British cutters from 1850 and 1885 as, while designers strove to improve hull form, construction and ballasting, sail plan design remained relatively stagnant. These yachts could be, and were, raced in very hard weather, when topmasts were usually housed and lower sails reefed and shifted. However, they sometimes lost bowsprits through bursting the bobstay and occasionally

Fig. 31 First class racing cutter *Vanduara*, 1880. Designed by G L Watson. Built by D W Henderson, Glasgow. Dimensions: 86 ft 1 in × 16 ft 2 in × 14 ft 6 in draught.

topmasts were carried away; both usually from pitching in a sea. When these racers were outclassed and converted to cruising the sail plan was reduced from *above*, not from each end. If it had been, probably a quarter century's progress might have been achieved at one step.

By the 1870s, materials were available to heighten rigs and steel wire came into general use for standing rigging, but change came slowly in the cutter rig. Rigging screws were still regarded with suspicion though they had been successfully used in the Plymouth cutter *Ada*, built in 1837, a prizewinner in south coast regattas for forty years before she was converted to a fishing smack at Brixham.

Sails improved in cut and quality. The leading yacht sailmakers were Messrs Lapthorn of Gosport and Charles Ratsey of Cowes, who advocated use of cotton sailcloth in Britain for many years until its superiority over flax in racing efficiency was at last recognised in the 1880s and became universal until the 1950s.

Several large racing cutters of the period were designed by Alexander Richardson, a Liverpool naval architect, including the 83 ft *Samaena* (1880), *Lorna* (1881), *Irex* 88 ft (1884) and *Iverna* (1890); the two last sailed by Captain William O'Neill of Kingstown, Ireland, with crews from Itchen. They were the last large craft built under the uninformed tonnage rule before it changed for the length and sail area rule which did not, at first, tax beam or depth, and resulted in a healthier type.

The 1890s brought tremendous upsurge of interest in British yachting in all classes from tiny half-raters to the largest racing cutters, four of which were ordered in the winter months of 1892. At Glasgow George Watson designed, and Hendersons built *Britannia* for the Prince of Wales and *Valkyrie II* for the Earl of Dunraven. William Fife III, at Fairlie, designed and built the unlucky *Calluna*, and at Southampton, J and G Fay's designer Joseph Soper worked all through the Christmas holidays draughting the beautiful *Satanita*, the fastest cutter on a reach ever built, sailing at over 16 knots on a timed course off the Isle of Wight. The four yachts were alike in general appearance and size. *Satanita*'s dimensions were 131 ft 6 in overall, 93 ft 6 in waterline × 24 ft 6 in beam × 14 ft 6 in draught. She displaced 126 tons. Her sail plan was the tallest but she typified the quartette. The newly permitted forward overhang shortened the bowsprit and enabled the forestay to be set further forward reducing the jib foot and improving its aspect. However, her total hoist to waterline length was still only 1·2, compared with the 1·14 of the eleven years older *Vanduara*. Total sail area was 10,094 square feet comprising: mainsail 5,264, headsails 3,360 and topsail 1,470. The boom was 91 ft long and height from deck to topmast shoulder 114 ft. In her second season *Satanita*'s sail plan was altered; 3 ft was docked from the boom, 5 ft from the bowsprit and 5 ft added to the gaff; and she improved her speed, averaging 13·7 knots from Gravesend, round the Mouse Light-vessel and back on a broad and close reach, over a much longer course than her previous higher speed.

The increased sail area and speed of these cutters resulted in many broken bowsprits and topmasts, and several sprung masts, for staying was lagging behind the rapid hull development. Their deeper and more concentrated ballast keels and greater beam, allowed by rule, improved power to carry sail and made designers look upwards.

It is an interesting fact that command of all four of these big class racers was offered to racing skippers from Rowhedge; such was then the fame in the yachting world of the Essex village of only 1,000 inhabitants. Thomas Jay sailed *Satanita*, William Cranfield *Valkyrie II*, and John Carter was offered command of both *Calluna* and *Britannia*, but chose the Royal cutter. So *Calluna* was sailed by Archie Hogarth from Port Bannatyne on the Clyde.

It was no mere chance which gained Colnesiders their reputation. Their subtle skill in racing stemmed from sailing the weatherly North Sea cutter smacks – a wonderful nursery for fore and aft seamen. These great Essex sailing masters were above all fine helmsmen, having a natural ability to windward, using excellent judgment, and were more than mere sail trimmers; they possessed the faculty of taking in hand and tuning up the whole fabric of hull and rig, besides concerting the efforts of a crew then numbering anything up to 50 hands. To succeed they had to act more quickly than their opponents, themselves equally experienced men; know the rules thoroughly, and have iron nerves when stretching them to their limits – for a major error of judgment at the helm would not only shatter a reputation but might cost the lives of several men. They were fine seamen, refined personalities in sole charge of these great yachts and their orders were carried out with an unquestioning smartness by crews of selected racing hands from the area.

William Cranfield raced *Valkyrie II* for the America's Cup in 1893 and in 1894, George Watson designed a new super-cutter for Dunraven's final challenge of 1895. The *Valkyrie III* was one of the most extreme racers ever built and her statistics are worth appreciation. Her dimensions were 129 ft overall, 88 ft 10 in lwl × 26 ft 2 in × 20 ft draught. She measured 187 ft from bowsprit end to boom end and carried a 77¾ ton lead keel. Construction was composite with elm bottom and teak topside planking. Sail area was 13,028 square feet. Mast, deck to head, 96 ft × 25 in diameter; boom 105 ft; gaff 69 ft; topmast 62 ft 6 in × 13½ in diameter; bowsprit 34 ft outboard × 16 in diameter. Five shrouds each side. One set of running backstays to the masthead, and one to the hounds, besides the shifting backstays to the topmast head (Fig. 32). She was the first large yacht to have a steel mast, but her wooden mast was stepped for the cup races. She was commanded by William Cranfield with a crew of 37 hands, mainly from Rowhedge.

During the next ten years sail areas continued to increase and steel masts and booms became common in large yachts, but sail plans crept upwards slowly. Gradually, topmasts were combined into the lower masts, as in *Shamrock III* of 1903 (14,000 square feet), designed by William Fife III, saving weight of topmast housing.

In 1896 Watson designed the splendid racing cutter *Meteor II* for Kaiser Wilhelm of Germany, who had previously owned the ex-British cutter *Thistle* which challenged for the America's Cup in 1887. The 238 ton *Meteor II* was built by Henderson's of Glasgow and commanded by Captain Robert Gomes of Gosport, Hampshire, with an English crew who

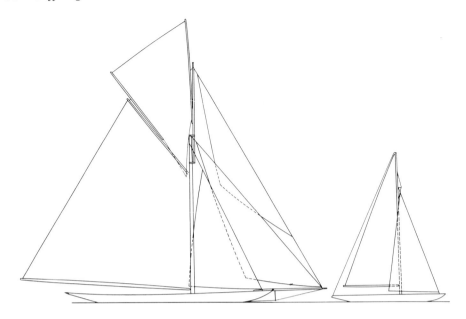

Fig. 32 Valkyrie III 1895 America's Cup challenger (left) compared with modern 12-metre yacht (right).
Valkyrie III dimensions: 129 ft overall × 88 ft 10 in waterline × 26 ft 2 in beam × 20 ft draught. Ordinary sail area 13,028 sq ft. Crew: *Valkyrie* – 37; 12-metre – 11.

were gradually replaced with Germans whom they taught yacht racing methods and tactics, later under Captain Ben Parker of Itchen.

When yacht racing 'went Metric' in 1906 and adopted the International Rule whose successor remains in use, gaff rig still dominated the sport. Classes were established from above 23 metres rating down to six metres, of which the 19 and 15 metres were the most handsome. However, there was detailed change in the cutter rig until 1912 when the leading contemporary designer, Charles Nicholson, of Camper and Nicholson, Gosport, produced the 15 metre cutter *Istria* for Sir Charles Allom. Always a weight-saver and original thinker, Nicholson scrapped the topsail yard by increasing the masthead to include topmast and topsail yard height in one spar of then extraordinary height. The topsail luff was set on this by track and slides. The long masthead was supported by two top forestays, opposed by a span leading to the shifter backstay. The peak halliards were set further up the masthead than usual to give a more efficient angle and the running backstay ended in a span to the hounds and opposed the forestay. This rigging and the extreme length of mast caused it to be known as Marconi rig, after the aerials of the radio inventor, then in the news. *Istria* was of large displacement on a short waterline and was unusually planked in Columbia spruce. Under Captain Alf Diaper of Itchen, she dominated the 15 metre class in 1912 and led to the use of Marconi rig by most subsequent gaff-rigged racing yachts.

Meanwhile, the big classes clung to gaff rig. Fife built the beautifully proportioned 90 ft cutter *Moonbeam* in 1920 for handicap racing under Captain Tom Skeats of Brightlingsea, Essex, and she won the King's Cup in 1920 and 1923. She came out with a yard topsail rig of 4,261 square feet to drive her 64 ton displacement hull. The continuing upward development of the cutter is illustrated by her bowsprit being only 9 ft outboard and the boom 2 ft over the counter. She changed to a Marconi mast which was soon fitted in the largest class British racing yachts, which had a grand revival and inspired the building in 1920 of the powerful big class racing cutter *Terpsichore*, designed by Herbert White and built by White Brothers of Itchen. She was the last large gaff rigged racer to be built and became better known as *Lulworth*, sailed by Captain Archie Hogarth, with a crew from the Clyde, Solent and Essex, who raced her against the King's old *Britannia*, Sir Thomas Lipton's 23 metre *Shamrock*, and the large schooners *Susanne* and *Westward*, until the bermudian rigged *Cambria* arrived in 1927 to finally prove the superiority of bermudian rig for big class racing.

Tom Diaper's Log

Tom Diaper
Tom Diaper's Log
first published 1950

Tom Diaper, whose grandfather was mentioned in the last extract, was a most successful professional skipper, with a career spanning the last years of the last century and the first half of this one. His log was published in 1950, when the company was still called Robert Ross Ltd (see Foreword). The minimum of alteration was made to the diaries, to retain as much as possible of the singular personality of the captain. This story makes an interesting comparison with that of Owen Parker, a member of one of the other famous families of Itchen which produced so many professional skippers. Extracts here include Diaper's account of the invention and naming of the spinnaker (compare it with John Leather's painstakingly researched version in the previous extract), a regatta on the Mediterranean and a trip to America for the America's Cup. He writes of the spinnaker:

'The first yacht my father took skipper of was the famous racing yacht Niobe. He was serving in a yacht called Destiny, when his father, who was at that time skipper of Niobe, died, and my father was asked to take his place. His age was then twenty-five, and the Niobe was the first yacht to set a spinnaker.

'A Mr Gordon was the inventor at the time. He owned the business of sailmaker at the bottom of High Street, Southampton, and my grandfather was the skipper. They took the yacht out to the English Channel and set and tried the spinnaker. There have been many who have asked why the sail was named spinnaker. This is how it was told to me by my father.

'When the sail was set and it billowed out to the breeze, one of the sailors said 'Now that is the sail to make her spin!' A gentleman on board took that phrase and reversed it to spinmaker, eventually shortening it to spinnaker, and so it is called today. All this is as it was told to me; I am open to correction.'

Now we come to the year 1900. It was the 7th of January, 1900, when I received a letter from Mr Buxenstein asking me to be in Berlin the 15th January, bringing my mate with me and leaving him in Hamburg in lodgings, while I went on to Berlin to get my instructions regarding what I was to do with the *Klein Polly*. So me and my mate travelled to Germany, via the London–Harwich to Hamburg route. Leaving the mate at Hamburg, I went onto Berlin and when I went to the boss's office he told me to go to the Mugglesee where the *Klein Polly* was laid up. He had already given the order to have the boat sent to Hamburg by the time I got there, to see if everything was in apple-pie order. When I arrived at Mugglesee Yard and inspected I found the boat was already on the train, all her gear as well. Everything was correct, and ready to leave for Max Oertz's Yacht Werft, Hamburg; so I returned to the office, got my instructions and everything to take the *Klein Polly* to the South of France.

I arrived at Hamburg before the boat, connected with my mate and the German chap Jack Hulberg. I had wired for him to meet me at Oertz's Yacht Werft from his home on Rugen Island in the Baltic, hoping the boat would arrive at the yard before the steam boat arrived what was to take her on board. The *Klein Polly* arrived at the yard the next day, so two days after the steamer arrived we was going to float her across the river Elbe to the steamer. But in the meantime it froze so hard that the river had frozen over. The ice was three inches thick and so much traffic had broken it up, and the tide running six miles an hour had so many ice floes that we decided to hire eight horses and a strong lorry to take the yacht round by road. We had to muffle the wheels with ropes and chains, the roads were so icy. We got her on board, lifting her by the heavy crane and got her properly secured. This steam boat was taking her as far as Havre. Then we was to put her on board a French Translantic ship to take her from Havre as far as Marseilles. We found on arriving at Havre that the other ship would not get there for another five days and the German steamship could not stay that long. So the crane took us off her deck and put us in the Dock Harbour. This being a case of waiting five days, and being on a Thursday, I left her in the dock-master's and the mate's hands and caught the night mailboat to Southampton, arriving home on Friday morning. My wife was surprised as she thought I was on the way to Marseilles. Anyhow I had two nights home, besides seeing Southampton beating Newcastle by one goal to nil at the Dell in the Cup.

I returned to Havre on Sunday night. The French steamer arrived on Tuesday morning. We put our boat on board and secured her properly by 12 noon and was told we ought to be on board by 7 p.m. for dinner.

Now I can say in the German boat from Hamburg we lived like lords, with four good meals a day and coffee first thing in the morning. But in the French boat we only had two meals a day and no coffee in the morning. Breakfast at 10 a.m. was a bottle of red wine and a loaf of bread, nothing else. For dinner we had a plate of soup as one course, about one ounce of meat for second course, and we had to eat that first before the third course, which consisted of a spoonful of cabbage. The fourth course was a potato – one, mind you, cut in halves; but we had a first-class cabin. I saw the captain and offered to pay five francs a day for each of us for extra food, but he said he would have done it, only he was frightened of the other captain. He told me the ship was a reserve ship and was double-manned with officers, from the captain down to the junior officer. I can tell you we was pleased when we got to the South of France.

When we were entering the port of Marseilles just at dark we saw a man in a row boat. We called him and we put a rope over the side and slid down it into the boat. He put us ashore and we found a café where we had a good feed of ham and eggs and coffee; and what a fill-out, for we were nearly starved! But I knew we should not have left the ship like that. We ought to have waited till the captain had cleared the ship and the port doctor had cleared her. We slept on shore that night, and, my! when we appeared on board there was trouble. Our German secretary was on board and he spoke French. He told me they was going to put us in gaol, but I explained all about it and told him I would never sail in a French ship again and he would have to put the *Klein Polly* on a German ship or an English one, for she was too small to sail back to Germany. Anyway the doctor run the rule over us and cleared us and they let us go free.

Well we got *Klein Polly* off the deck into the water and a small boat towed us round to the yacht harbour, where we moored her stern on to the quay. We went and engaged lodgings at the Sailors' Home for the three of us. So after a night's rest we went down to the harbour and rigged *Klein Polly* and made her ready for racing. We had three days racing at Marseilles, taking all three first prizes. Then we left for Cannes, raced there, then at Nice and Monte Carlo. We started in twenty-two races. We broke our main boom one day at Cannes and on another day at Cannes we carried away our mast. Of course we had to be towed to the harbour.

Now the boss said we had a spare mast and asked where it was. I said it was at Nice as I could not get a conveyance at Marseilles to drop it at Cannes. Nice, twenty miles further east was the nearest place where I could get it sent. I said we would have to hire horses and a lorry to bring it from Nice by road to the dock. So he said 'Being as I can speak French I will go with you, in the train. We race again tomorrow. Do you hope to be ready?'

I said 'Yes, I want to surprise the boats in our class.'

So we took the train at 4 p.m., got to Nice and saw the broker who had charge of the spars, two sets in two forty-five feet-long cases. We hired six horses and a lorry, saw the cases put on the lorry, then the boss called the lorry man to him. The boss took out of his pocket a gold twenty franc piece. Showing it to the driver he said, 'The captain will give you this if you are at the beach end of the Cannes harbour by five minutes to 12 midnight.' It was 7.30 p.m. when all was ready to start. The boss gave me the gold piece and we left by train and returned to Cannes.

There were several yachts from my home village of Itchen. Their crews offered to help, so we went to the beach end at 11.45 p.m. and the lorry arrived at 11.52 p.m., eight minutes before the appointed hour of midnight. So I gave the driver the gold twenty francs; and pleased? I should say he was!

We unloaded the lorry and all promised to be at that spot at 4 o'clock in the morning. We surprised our class when they saw us sailing around pulling everything in place. The Frenchmen knew that I had ordered a new mast to be made, and as they knew it could not be made in time for the race that day, of course they wanted to know how we secured a new mast.

We raced that day and won the first prize. Altogether we got twenty first prizes and only lost on the two days we had the accidents. I think the following copy of the testimony will finish 1900 well.

Copy of Testimony, Berlin, 21st December, 1900.

Mr Thomas Diaper of Itchen Ferry has acted during the two summers of 1899 and 1900 as master of the German racing yacht, Polly, *30 tons T.M., also during the winter racing season 1899–1900 in the Mediterranean as master of the racing yacht* Klein Polly, *both yachts owned by me. I will testify very willingly that Mr Diaper fulfilled all his duties as a racing skipper and master of the crew in a very satisfactory way. He did his best to maintain discipline, cleanliness and general good conduct of the crew. He kept both yachts smart, tidy and clean, and yacht conditions and the drill of his crew was always admired at yachting stations in Germany, Denmark, Sweden and France. Mr Diaper himself was always willing to fulfil the owner's requests in a good manner and he has always acted very skilfully at the tiller lines when racing, both yachts always being at the top of the class. I wish him cheerfully a similar good success in his further career as master of a racing yacht.*

Signed: GEORG BUXENSTEIN

That ends 1900

★   ★   ★

For 1920 I had shipped in the *Shamrock* twenty-three-metre as second mate under my brother, Alf Diaper, who was the skipper of her. We started on the 15th February to make her ready to cross the Atlantic to act as trial-horse to train and tune up the *Shamrock IV* which was already over there. She went over in 1914, only the war came on. The *Shamrock* twenty-three-metre was not one of the *Shamrocks* built for the American

Cup, but built to race around the British coast regattas, so, as I said, we started to make ready.

The *Shamrock* twenty-three-metre was over at Camper & Nicholson's yard. Jim Gilby, the mate, was getting her ready with the port watch for the crossing under her ocean rig. She was being made into yawl rig for the crossing, while I, the second mate, with the starboard watch, was cleaning and making and packing all her racing gear – sails, spars, and all the halyards, etc. – and labelling it to go across in one of the Cunard boats; we had to take the weight of everything. Quite a big job it is to pack a twenty-three-metre racing gear, but we managed to get it done by the 1st April, and the *Shamrock* was launched and towed out of the river. The compass was adjusted and we moored off Southampton on the Test.

The day after next, 3rd April, all hands went on shore and signed on to take *Shamrock* twenty-three-metre to America and bring her back to Southampton after the races for the America's Cup, whether they were won or lost, if required to do so. We left Southampton 5th April and let go anchor off Yarmouth, Isle of Wight, for the night to catch a fair ebb-tide through the Needles passage, for the wind was dead against us all the way down the English Channel. We left Yarmouth the morning of the 7th April, 1920, and sure enough had the wind ahead the whole way down to Falmouth, where we put in and anchored so that we might do some little alterations what wanted doing for the passage across. It was well for us we had done so, for that night it came on to blow a very hard gale, continuing for almost a fortnight. Then the gale fined down to a light wind. We left Falmouth and had got about thirty miles to the south-west of Land's End, when the gale came on with redoubled fury. So we ran back to Falmouth again. On the fourth day in there, we made another start, the wind still hanging in the west. We made the first leg of our journey to Ushant, when we put her on the other tack, standing off to make a good clearance of that dangerous point, the wind beginning to increase and the sea getting up. We kept tacking her up to the windward till the third night out of Falmouth, no one getting any rest, it was so rough. On this third night out I went on watch at 12 o'clock midnight, I had just relieved them when an able-seaman asked me to take a look around the forecastle. I did, and quickly got the captain and navigator to look also. This is what I saw. An iron stanchion in the centre of the forecastle, which was a deck support, was starting to bend, which should not have been, but the pounding of her long bow and the heavy seas pounding her deck was causing that – and not only that. The fishplate what ran around each side of the ship, underneath the covering board, was half-inch steel plating and it was bending the port and starboard in line across the deck with the iron stanchion, all in a line bending together. Myself, having had more than anyone on board of sea-going, in that class of ship, warned them that if we kept on pounding her bow in such a storm much longer, the *Shamrock* would not reach America.

Why not then turn back and wait for a better chance of luck and a fair wind? The skipper and navigator together said, 'We dare not turn back for Sir Thomas Lipton wants this boat in America.'

I myself answered, 'To h— with Sir Thomas! He looked out for himself not to be here with us. There are twenty-two of us on board, and sixty-eight in England depending on us. What will they all do if we are lost? The owner cannot look after them, and you know the boats is no good to save us. Now will you listen to me this once, for I have had a lot of experience in this kind of craft. It is 12.20 and I will try to keep her going until 2 a.m., and if it is no better by then I will turn her round and make for the first port we can reach in safety. The only way you will get this boat to America is by running away from it now in this storm. I will take the blame, if there is any.' So that was agreed on. They went below, being worn out by their long watch on deck in the gale. The strain had told on the skipper who was ill; it was physically impossible for him to carry on longer on deck. At fifteen minutes before 2 a.m., I called an able seaman, saying, 'Go below, see the first mate, tell him to get all hands out and make ready to turn the ship round.'

'Now, you, Jim,' I said, 'go forward to the main rigging. Have a rope put around you for safety and when I call out to you, you will be looking for a dark spot in the waves. Call out like hell, "A dark spot, Tom." Then I will, if I have enough way on and the ship answers all right, lee-ho, and every man for himself.'

So only a short space of time had gone by, and I had offered up a short prayer, for guidance and safety in the job I was going to do – the same as I had always done since I started going to sea, to the only One up above Who can see you safely through anything, good or danger, if you ask Him – when the mate's voice came, 'A dark spot coming, Tommy.'

'All right,' I answered, 'and every man for himself.'

Now every man was at his station and everything went just like clock-work. We got that ship round, in spite of the mountainous seas and a hurricane of wind and dark as a dungeon, as well as if we were on a mill-pond, without shipping a pail of water, or breaking a rope yarn. That was the time that Sir Thomas Lipton ought to have been with us, trying to cross the Atlantic. So having got her round, I set the course north-east, and went below to report to the navigator the course and distance on the log, and had put the oil bags over. Then, turning to the captain I said, 'I don't think a tot of whisky would hurt the men. It will act like medicine. I will enter it in the official log as such.'

'Well, Tom,' he said, 'I reckon you all deserve it; you all done a good job. I nearly thought I had got into the Solent.'

But I answered, 'It was a bit too jumpy to think that! But we had a lucky turning.' We drank our tot and then the watch below turned in, or lay down somewhere to try and get some rest. I returned to my watch on deck, but, owing to the wind veering more to the west and making the heavy seas coming more on the quarter, we could not make a true north-easterly course for Falmouth. The navigator was a bit worried, and the skipper too, but I said, 'We shall make Dartmouth, what's the odds? We can get repairs done there.' For when we did get there we looked a proper wreck on deck. The lashings had pulled the stem-pieces away from the two eighteen-foot lifeboats, all the plank ends had pulled away from the stems, and both boats had to be made seaworthy.

We stayed till the repairs were finished in about a week, repairing the mainsail which we had partly blown away, and then we made a fresh start from which we did not turn back.

From the Azores to New York we had two separate moderate gales lasting twelve hours each with light variable winds in between. But the gales were with us, and they drove us about twelve knots – not bad, loaded down like we were, fully rigged.

We reached New York. At the entrance the Customs cleared us and we were towed to City Point, New York Yacht Yard, where the yard went to work to change the ocean gear into the racing gear, that had arrived out long before we got there. We were in them in a week, all but the topmast. We had to leave that on deck; with it up in place we was one hundred and seventy-five feet from the deck to the top of the topmast, too tall to go under Brooklyn Bridge. We were soon ready to help tune up the *Shamrock IV*. We had some races together. She had three out of five against us, but she did not win the cup – too many amateur sailing masters. In fact I have before me now a photograph out of a New York newspaper with the *Resolute* catching the *Shamrock* up quick, when it ought to be the other way about – the *Shamrock* leaving the *Resolute* behind. The *Shamrock* lost the cup where she ought to have won it. In fact, Sir Thomas Lipton and Lord Delaware came on our *Shamrock* on 27th November, and said he had done wrong to lose the cup. Our crew was the one that ought to have been on *Shamrock IV*. He would have taken any odds on it, but he found out too late.

So they decided to lay *Shamrock* twenty-three-metre up at City Point, and send both crews home.

So that ends a bit of adventure going to America to see an English yacht bring the cup away, but they will never do it the way they try too many captains. All that is needed to race a yacht, is one captain, with one crew, one timekeeper, and one pilot. Two or three guests, but no one to interfere with the captain – without he is going to hit another boat, that should be pointed out.

The Fastnet Gales of 1957

K Adlard Coles
Heavy Weather Sailing
first published 1967

Heavy Weather Sailing *is undoubtedly one of the outstanding books in the list. The accounts of small boats in
gales and lessons drawn from them make compelling reading.
The author writes:*

'*The purpose of my book* Heavy Weather Sailing *was to
give practical descriptions of the experiences of yachts
caught out in heavy weather and gales, to make research
into the meteorological conditions (especially of the fac-
tual rather than estimated wind forces) and to give the
lessons drawn from each. Happily, the sea remains the sea
while everything else changes at an ever-increasing rate,
so there has been little to alter in the book itself.*

'*It is difficult for me as author to select the most suitable extract from my book as some of the most dramatic
occurrences in ocean storms were contributed by other
sailing men. However, if the choice is to be limited to my
own experiences, I think* The Fastnet Gales of 1957, *in
which there were some 70 per cent retirements, was one of
the most eventful. Moreover, it took place at a time when
the rating rules were relatively static, before the period of
frequent alteration and development.*

'*As to modern ocean racers I cannot give an authori-
tative opinion, as over ten years ago I lowered my racing
colours for the last time. I can only generalise. I am impressed by the remarkable achievements and seamanship
displayed in the Round the World races and, at the other
end of the size scale, by the almost incredible speed of
some of the modern Half-Tonners in heavy weather. These
seem to combine the minimum weight in their light-
displacement hulls with the maximum strength conferred
by scientific design and construction. Being old-fashioned
I cannot say that I consider many of the new racing*

designs to be kindly to the eye but, to be fair, if one wants beauty in sail one has to go back to the pre-war ocean racers such as Latifa *and* Bloodhound *and to the designers Fife, C E Nicholson and others.*

'*In conclusion, turning to the cruising side of sailing, I think that most of the ocean racers of around 1957 vintage, with their comparatively long keels and relative steadiness on the helm, offered the great advantage of providing first-rate cruising yachts with little or no alteration.*'

The Fastnet Race has a reputation for bad weather. Like the races to Spain, it starts on the last Saturday of Cowes week, early in August, and as often as not there is half a gale from the south-west blowing on that particular day.

The Fastnet is essentially a windward race along the South Coast, and when one has beaten as far as Land's End, often against a gale for part of the way, and has passed through the gap between the Longships and the Seven Stones light-vessel into St George's Channel (which for convenience I will call the Irish Sea) the wind may suddenly veer to provide a beat of another 180 miles dead to windward to the Fastnet Rock. Once round this turning mark there is usually a lively reach, or a run, over the remaining 230 miles round the Bishop Rock off the Scilly Isles to finish at Plymouth. As the late American authority, Alfred Loomis, put it: 'If the Fastnet isn't an ocean race, it has all the worst features of such a contest plus mental hazards that have to be experienced to be fully appreciated.'

But the Fastnet is not always rough. It can be so calm that the betting would be on a 14 ft International dinghy if the rules permitted one to enter. So it was in the years when I entered *Cohoe II*. With her cut-down rig she was sluggish in light airs and we were lucky to finish even in the first half of the fleet.

In 1956 (the year of the record Channel gale) I sold *Cohoe II*, and placed an order for a faster all-round boat which we named *Cohoe III*. She was built at Poole by Newman & Sons Ltd., and designed, like her predecessor, by Charles A Nicholson. Her dimensions were 32·6 ft overall, 26 ft L.W.L., 9·1 ft beam and 6 ft draught. Like *Cohoe II*, she was an example of cod's head, mackerel tail hull with a fine run aft below water. Although 2 ft 5 in shorter overall than *Cohoe II*, she was much bigger, as she ended in a wide transom stern which in some respects is akin to having a larger yacht and chopping the counter off. Compared with the original *Cohoe*, of about equal length overall and on the waterline, she was more than double the size and displaced about 8 tons. She was a sloop with a sail area of 533 sq ft as designed, but when I later converted her to masthead rig set to a tubular stainless steel bowsprit this was increased to 615 sq ft. The features of the new yacht were her stiffness and sail-carrying ability in hard weather and her roominess and strength. Everything about her construction, whether hull, mast or rigging, was above average strength and her coachroof was stiffened with steel. All this involved some sacrifice of speed, but I had hoped to sail her over for the Bermuda Race, and I remembered Humphrey Barton's advice about deck structures after his *Vertue XXXV* was nearly sunk in the Atlantic. Short-ended and sturdy looking, *Cohoe III* was one of the most powerful and durable small sea-going yachts ever built.

The first Fastnet Race she entered was in 1957 and it ran true to form, for it was said to be one of the roughest in Fastnet history. I had with me as crew Ross, Alan Mansley, Patrick Madge and Peter Nicholson, the son of the designer and a brilliant helmsman.

Forty-one yachts crossed the starting line at Cowes on Saturday morning, 10 August, in really dirty weather. It was described as a south-westerly gale. Force 8 was reported at the Scillies and Force 6 and 7 at two neighbouring inland weather stations. *Cohoe III* started under staysail and had a few turns rolled in her mainsail, so, although it was said she was carrying relatively more sail than others, I do not think the wind force could have been more than 25 to 30 knots (Force 6 to 7), gusting perhaps 40 knots.

The conditions suited *Cohoe III*, and she quickly took the lead in her class, and by the time she had reached the Needles she had overhauled many of the Class II and Class I yachts. With the ebb stream against the SW wind the Solent was a mass of short breaking seas and the racing fleet took a dusting. I expected a big sea off the Needles, over the Bridge where the English Channel is entered and the seas build up as the tearing ebb tide meets the full force of a south-westerly. The seas proved big and broken, but not dangerous, and as *Cohoe III* smashed her way into the open Channel the waves lengthened and speed improved. Nevertheless, it was

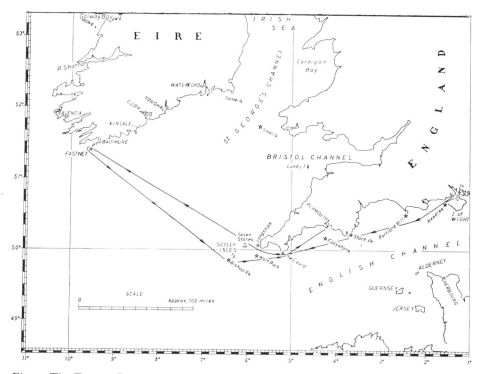

Fig. 33 The Fastnet Course.

hard going in dirty conditions with rain and flying spray adding to the poor visibility.

Tack by tack and watch by watch *Cohoe III* beat her way westwards throughout the day, with her crew half blinded by flying spray, so that the helmsmen took short spells at the tiller turn by turn.

By the late evening *Cohoe III* in a mass of spray had beaten across Bournemouth Bay, past St Alban's Head, which was shrouded in driving rain, and had arrived off Portland, where she just missed her tide, with *Myth of Malham* and another yacht within sight ahead. The tides were springs, and with 4 knots against us our speed over the bottom slowed down, and before long night fell upon us. On deck all was dark except the friendly orange glow of the compass and the reflections of the navigation lights. The cold regular four white flashes of Portland Bill lay on our starboard bow. The watch on deck were secured by safety harness, and they needed it, for every sea broke aboard forward, and in the gusts the yacht lay far over.

Down below the aft end of the cabin was like a half-tide rock. As each sea struck the cabin top forward it came streaming aft, flooding through the aft hatch and a cabin door which had broken, as that year we had no spray hood. Both quarter berths were flooded and the chart table unusable, so I had to spread the sodden chart on the table at the forward end of the saloon.

Navigation was a whole-time job as we were skirting Portland Race, with the spare man on deck taking hand bearings on Portland Lighthouse. It was also physically difficult, as I was thrown about so much. If the chart was left for a moment it would shoot across the cabin together with the parallel rulers and dividers on to the lee berth. Progress was desperately slow, as it always is when rounding a light, but hour by hour the bearing changed and I was able to plot each position a little west of the last one.

Regularly the yacht needed pumping. Masses of water found its way into the bilges. The seas must have been getting through the cracks edging the cockpit lockers, and spray through the cabin hatch, through the broken cabin door, and through the ventilators. It is extraordinary how much water gets below during gales and it has been the same with all my yachts, even with *Cohoe IV*, which had a fibreglass hull which cannot possibly leak. We had two pumps, but the one in use was situated in the cabin with a long hose which was led into the cockpit so that the water returned to the sea via the self-emptying drains. I took it in turns with the spare man to man the pump. It was tiring work and a joy each time that the water subsided and the pump sucked dry.

Only one man remained on deck at a time except when taking bearings, for it is a mistake to expose two to the flying spray and the cold of the night for longer than necessary. The watches were four-hourly, but the spells at the helm off Portland were fifteen minutes only. On release from the tiller the spare man would hurry below to light a cigarette to add to the fumes of my own cigarettes as I worked on the charts. There was a record fug. As Peter was the only non-smoker, he must have suffered a lot, but he never complained.

Cohoe III did not slam when working to windward in rough water as did *Annette* and to a lesser extent *Cohoe I*. But off Portland Bill, thrashing to windward at 6 knots, she would very occasionally fall irregularly in a wave formation and come down on her stem with a most dreadful shock. The whole ship shuddered, the saucepans rattled and the teapot would be thrown off the gimballed stove. This was not a matter of ordinary, regular pounding as is found in many yachts, but it was the effect of nearly 8 tons weight of boat throwing herself at 6 knots over the head of a big sea and falling on her stem at a sharp angle on water that sounded as hard as a pavement. In the saloon one wondered how timber construction could stand such treatment, and after each impact I would lift the cabin floor-boards to check whether there was an inrush of water resulting from damage forward, but my anxiety was uncalled for. Peter remarked that he thought for this sort of work an ocean racer should be double-diagonal planked.

As we soldiered on against both wind and tide progress seemed desper-ately slow, but inch by inch we edged through off the tail of the race and by the midnight change of watch we had broken through and lay about 2 miles to the SW of Portland.

Shortly after midnight, when the new watch had taken over, I was called on deck, as the helmsman thought the yacht was carrying too much sail. When I took the tiller I found that he was right. The wind had freshened to Force 8 (34–40 knots) gusting higher in the squalls, and though the yacht was sailing grandly she was hard pressed and there was a risk of things carrying away.

It was time to shorten sail. Patrick and Peter rolled the mainsail down, bringing the peak to the upper spreaders, the staysail was lowered and the storm jib set. All this was done as smartly as if in daylight in the Solent. Alas! The yacht was now over-reefed and I had forgotten that the storm jib (roped all round), inherited from *Cohoe II*, was cut too full to be of service as a racing sail. *Cohoe III* sagged badly to leeward and there are unlighted buoys to the west of Portland Bill. Under reduced sail we could no longer clear them and it was improbable that they would be spotted in the dark in time to avoid collision. Thus, we were forced to come on to starboard tack, bringing the weakening foul tide on our beam and thus losing much of the distance that had been so hard earned.

I have clear impressions in my memory of that outward tack. The moon appeared between the clouds flying overhead and at times the yacht and sea were bathed in light. The seas were high, but under reduced sail the boat was an easy match for them. A yacht passed close ahead of us, running east under bare poles, her port light shining brightly. A lifeboat also passed on the same course.

We tacked 5 miles out and I then handed over and turned in. Both quarter berths were flooded out, so I took the root berth in the fo'c'sle, which is supposed to be untenable in a gale. At each plunge of the boat I felt I was left in the air and put my hand up to prevent being struck by the deck above. Sleep was out of the question, though I managed to get a modest degree of much-needed rest.

The wind moderated in the early hours of the following morning (Sunday, 11th), falling to Force 7 and, after the change of watch, the staysail was reset and some of the turns in the mainsail were let out. It remained rough going in driving rain over forlorn grey seas the whole way across Lyme Bay, but we made better progress with more sail. To cut a long story short, the overreefing west of Portland Bill lost us a lot of time, for it caused us to miss our tide at Start Point. I put into Dartmouth for shelter during the foul tide. This gave us the opportunity to get a hot meal on a level table and with the aid of two primuses to dry the interior of the yacht somewhat and masses of wet clothes.

More important, it enabled us to carry out a number of small but useful repairs. Some of the screws in the mast track were beginning to work loose and had to be screwed up, repairs were made to the broken cabin door and I nailed canvas across the aft end of the coachroof and hatch to keep some of the water out of the quarter berths and chart table.

Once in shelter there is sometimes a reluctance to put to sea again, but on this occasion there was no delay, thanks partly to Alan, who kept us up to the mark. We left early on the tide and got past Start Point close to the rocks in the early slack. The wind had moderated and next morning (Monday, 12th) we sighted *Elseli IV*, the Swedish entry which rated at the top of the class. The race was on again and over the remaining 500 miles of the course was bitterly contested, the two yachts rarely being out of sight of each other.

West of the Lizard the wind went light and *Elseli IV*, with her big masthead rig, gained on us steadily tack by tack. She had left us far astern by the time she had rounded Land's End.

Luckily for *Cohoe III*, the wind freshened again, and we found ourselves hard on the wind for much of the 180-mile stretch across the Irish Sea. The wind was about Force 6 to Force 7 (some say Force 8), so it was a tough passage pressed under staysail and whole mainsail. Both yachts arrived off the Irish coast on Wednesday morning, 14th, almost at the same time. Meanwhile the wind had veered to the north-west and headed us, so that our landfall was some 20 miles east of the Fastnet, whereas the bigger yachts had been able to fetch the rock on one tack.

We scored a few miles off *Elseli IV* by standing in on the Irish coast and tacking inside the Stag Rocks, thus getting an earlier fair tide and smoother water under the lee of the land. Off Baltimore we all looked longingly towards the soft contours of Ireland lying so alluringly close on the starboard hand, but there was little time for such idle thoughts, for *Elseli IV* was not far astern, and by the time we had rounded the Fastnet Rock at 1340 she was snapping at *Cohoe III*'s heels.

The run of 150 miles from the Fastnet Rock to the Bishop provided closely contested racing between the two yachts. *Elseli IV* had lost her spinnaker boom, but running under mainsail and boomed-out genoa she gained on us and steered a straighter course. *Cohoe III* carried all sail with her biggest spinnaker bellying out against the light blue sky and the dark blue white-crested seas. At 1610 we gybed and with an increasing wind she became almost unmanageable at times in the big quartering seas, forcing her to tack downwind too much to the westward. But for two hours she logged over 8 knots, far in excess of the maximum theoretical speed of a short-ended boat of only 26 ft waterline. For a while *Elseli IV* must have done better, for her log showed a steady 8 or 9 knots, and when surfing the needle was up to 11 knots. Gustav Plym describes the surfing in his book *Yacht and Sea* as 'really fantastic and something that none of us had ever experienced before in such a relatively large boat . . . it was fascinating and, to tell the truth – slightly terrifying'.

At nightfall *Cohoe III* lowered her spinnaker and set her genoa. It was blowing hard at a good Force 7, and higher in the gusts and the seas were building up. The night was rough and at 0515 next morning all hands were called to gybe on to an easterly course for the Bishop Rock. This was a tricky job in the seas which Gustav Plym described as 'high breaking mountains of water', because of the weight of the wind in the full mainsail and the risk of breaking something or broaching as the boom went over, but the crew managed it smartly.

When dawn came there was no sight of *Elseli IV* as we raced eastward. The wind had if anything increased, for it was blowing a good Force 7, possibly Force 8, and was reported as being Force 9. *Cohoe III*'s speed had risen again to over 8 knots. This was fortunate, because the two adversaries met again just west of the Bishop. *Elseli IV* had lost time when two hanks of her mainsail broke, and she reduced sail to avoid being pooped, but she had steered direct as compared with *Cohoe III*'s involuntary tacking downwind. There was a tremendous sea in the overfalls west of the Bishop, for here there was the full fetch of the Atlantic into a weather-going tide. The seas were positively tumultuous. *Elseli IV* was being driven through it all out. She made a spectacular sight and at times was almost lost to sight in the waves. Gustav Plym, her owner, told me afterwards that she broached-to twice, but neither yacht suffered any harm.

The seas were lower south of the Scillies and the gale gradually moderated throughout the day on the 80-mile run to Plymouth, though a gale warning was repeated at noon. Off Land's End the wind had softened sufficiently to enable *Cohoe III* to reset her spinnaker. *Elseli IV* could not respond owing to the loss of her spinnaker boom, and thus *Cohoe III* crossed the line with a lead of half an hour to win Class III by four hours on corrected time.

It had been a great battle between the British and the Swedish yacht which proved to be the only two small-class yachts left in the race. *Elseli IV*'s owner (Gustav Plym) was elected 'Yachtsman of the Year' in Sweden and I received a similar honour in Great Britain.

Captain John Illingworth's *Myth of Malham* won Class II, but the first place overall in the race was won by the Class I American yawl *Carina*. It was a fine achievement on the part of her owner, Dick Nye, and his crew, for when emerging early in the race from the Solent into the Channel at the Bridge buoy, *Carina* fell off a sea and suffered considerable structural damage forward and her staysail tack parted. As *Carina* crossed the finish line at the end of the race her owner remarked: 'All right, boys, we're over now; let her sink.' I admire his spirit.

Conclusions

Mr J A N Tanner, at that time the meterological correspondent of *Yachting World*, says that the Fastnet Race of 1957 was sailed in variable conditions brought about by two depressions. On Friday, the day before the start, a deepening depression (982 millibars compared with 976 millibars in the Santander gale of 1947 and the Channel gale of 1956) was moving eastwards. At the start of the race on Saturday it was moving up the Western Approaches, with another trough about 300 miles astern, the winds in this phase being even stronger than those which had gone before. The boisterous conditions continued for thirty-six hours and were followed by light and variable winds during Monday and the early part of Tuesday. The next depression (992 millibars) came in from west of Ireland and the wind set in from the north-west on Wednesday 'sufficiently boisterous to say that the race which started in a gale, also ended in one, and with nothing much different in between'.

Out of the forty-one starters in all classes only twelve completed the course. *Galloper* lost a man overboard. He had come on deck without a lifeline to empty a gash bucket and a sudden lurch sent him over the side. The one lifebelt thrown was so light that it was blown downwind too fast for him to get it, but he was able to secure a hold on the second buoy which was a heavy, sodden one of horseshoe type. It was only by superb seamanship under such wild conditions that he was rescued.

Inschallah had her deck-house ports stove in by a sea some 2 miles off Portland Bill and after exhibiting distress signals was escorted by the lifeboat into Weymouth Harbour. Maybe this was the yacht we had passed off Portland. *Maze* had the swaged end pulled out of a lower shroud and was

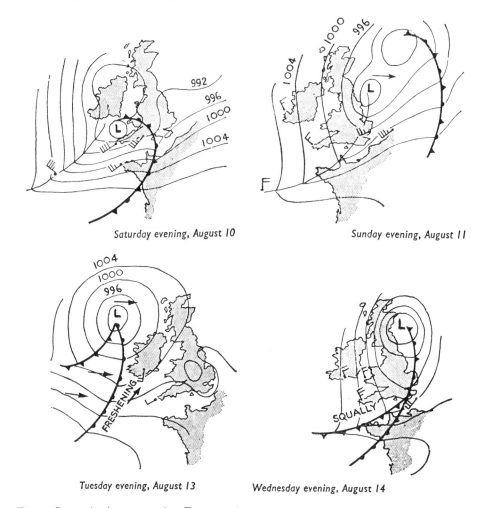

Saturday evening, August 10

Sunday evening, August 11

Tuesday evening, August 13

Wednesday evening, August 14

Fig. 34 Synoptic charts covering Fastnet gales, 1957.

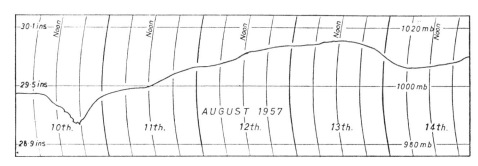

Fig. 35 Barograph trace, Fastnet Race, 1957.

dismasted. *Evenlode* incurred damage to her rudder, five of *Drumbeat's* winches broke under the strain and *Santander* developed a serious leak, found later to be due to a fractured keel bolt. Broken stays and torn sails were common and accounted for some of the retirements, but no doubt the principal cause was the old seafaring malady of sea-sickness. Lessons learnt were:

1. *Man overboard.* The accident in *Galloper* illustrates that personal lifelines are needed even for temporary visits to the deck, when driving to windward against gales. A sea must have struck *Galloper* on the windward side and I suspect that her crewman was catapulted overboard just as Geoff and I were in the Santander Race. The lee side of the cockpit is particularly dangerous and crew members coming up from below to empty the gash bucket or in a rush to avoid being sick in the cabin often forget their lifelines, which are laborious to don. The experience also suggests that two kinds of lifebuoy are required, light ones for use in ordinary conditions and a heavy one for use in high winds. Alternatively a lifebuoy should be attached to a small drogue.

2. *Damage.* Long periods of beating into gales find out any weaknesses in hull, rig, sails and gear. Moderate winds prevail in most ocean races and hence some designers tend to keep everything above deck as light as possible. This lightness pays in ordinary racing, but a considerable factor of safety is required for punching to windward through gales of this kind.

3. *Pounding and falling off a wave.* In the old International metre classes the hull form was given to pounding and they did not appear to suffer much as a result. Ocean racers with their shorter ends suffer less from this complaint, but when they do so the shock is, or appears to be much greater. John Illingworth in his book *Offshore* remarks that 'one wonders that every fastening in the boat is not loosened', but he adds 'the worst you are likely to do is to disturb the caulking in the forward part of the boat'. John Illingworth should know, because nobody has longer experience or drives a boat harder, but his ocean racers are designed and built for the job of hard racing.

Furthermore, there is a difference between pounding and what is called 'falling off a wave'. That is, breaking through the crest of a big sea at 6 to 7 knots so that the yacht literally falls into the trough on her stem. It was this that caused structural damage to *Carina*. A similar mishap occurred when *Bloodhound* fell off a wave off Berry Head. The impact damaged her stem scarf and caused a leak. She hove-to until dawn, when the extent of the damage could be identified, and she was able to carry on in the race, pumping only every four hours. *Elseli IV* broke three frames off Portland and it was thought that she had broken seven planks, but the damage was later found to be limited to surface splits at the nail-heads. Other yachts suffered damage, and it was this 'falling off a wave' that caused me occasional anxiety in *Cohoe III*. Much depends on the helmsman, who must luff to the crests and bear away at the top to let the boat down lightly in the trough. With a good man at the wheel the watch below will be able to relax, but with an inexperienced helmsman the impacts with waves will be terrific, enough to crack the heads in the fo'c'sle. The boat should be kept weaving in the seas, dancing all the time in the zest of it.

It used to be said that a yacht could take more punishment than her crew, but nowadays it is possible that with picked crew regularly relieved, and able to drive a yacht all out against gales, damage can result. It is no longer certain that the ship is stronger than her crew. The forward sections of an ocean racer and such matters as the scarf, frames and keel bolts certainly merit special consideration on the part of the designer.

4.   *Sheltering*. No cruising man, if he is in his right senses, will continue to beat to windward for long in Force 8 if shelter is at hand. Ocean racers have to plug on, but I think it sometimes pays to shelter, as *Cohoe III* did, rather than beat round a headland against a strong foul spring tide. If one takes the strength of the foul stream as lasting four hours all one has to do is to calculate the distance it will set the yacht back according to the tidal atlas and compare it with the distance likely to be made good tacking at a wide angle to the wind on account of rough seas, surface drift and leeway. The answer depends upon the size, design and stability of the individual boat, but if little is to be gained by keeping at sea it may pay in a long race to give a respite to the crew, provided no time is lost in getting under way again when the stream weakens.

The Sea

These pictures are part of a series taken by Captain Theo de Lange, some of which are included in Heavy Weather Sailing. *They are taken in North Atlantic gales of about Force 10/11. Many times we read descriptions of awesome seas, but these clear, sharp photographs of extreme conditions have a much more startling impact.*

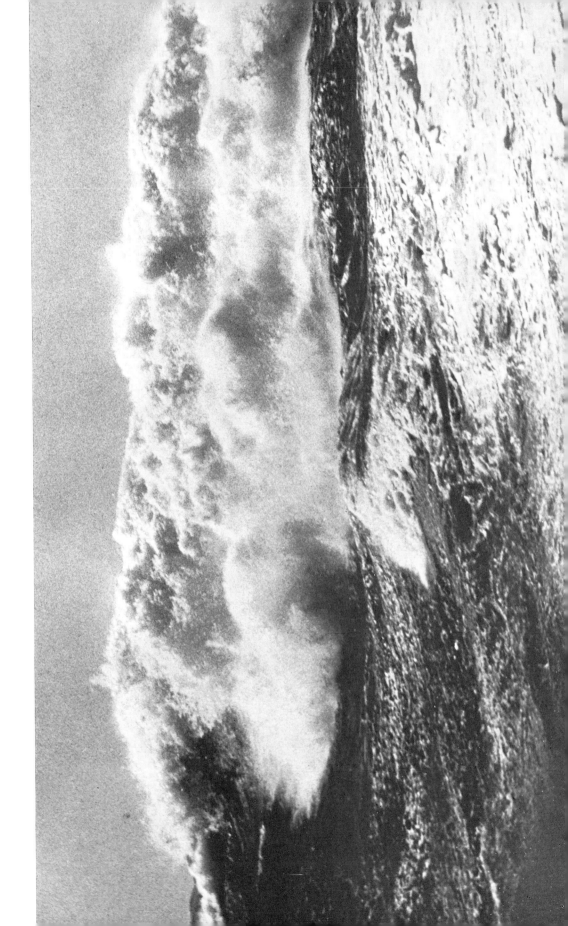

The Admiral's Cup, 1971

Owen Parker
Tack Now, Skipper
first published 1979

Owen Parker's story, Tack Now, Skipper, *recounts the career of a professional skipper or sailing master from the fifties to the present day. He is now, of course, Sailing Master on Edward Heath's* Morning Cloud, *and the description of a major campaign makes interesting comparison with similar memories by Tom Diaper in his day. The author writes:*

'*I was interested to read John Illingworth's thoughts on the Sydney–Hobart race which, of course, he won in 1945, the first time it was ever held. As it happens, it's just as well we didn't have a copy of his book on board* Morning Cloud *in 1969, because he comes down on the side of sticking to the rhumb line as against going off in search of wind or set. Perversely, it was finding the set which helped us to become only the second British boat ever to win the race. So, when I was asked to select an extract for this anthology, I was tempted to go for my chapter on the Sydney–Hobart.*

'*But the Admiral's Cup has an attraction which is hard to ignore, and this is what I have chosen. I hope it will evoke in the reader some of the thrills the racing offers the competitor as he sails for his country.*'

The Admiral's Cup is competed for in a series of races organised by the Royal Ocean Racing Club in British waters, every alternate year to co-incide with the Fastnet race, which culminates the series. The trophy is therefore contested in odd years, and this is arranged so as not to conflict with the similar Onion Patch series which is staged in America in even years, finishing with the Bermuda Race. The Onion Patch is the name by which Americans affectionately know this British island 500 miles off their eastern seaboard. Countries enter teams of three boats, and the Admiral's Cup, which was only started in 1957, has quickly become the major trophy as far as the British ocean racing man is concerned, if not the European and American; the honour of making the national team is highly coveted, with owners building boats specially designed to catch the selectors' eye.

Candidate for the Team

After we had done so well in the Sydney–Hobart race, the germ formed in Mr Heath's mind that he would like to try for the Admiral's Cup team. The crew had a number of meetings to discuss this early in 1970, so we all knew what was happening, and so that each could decide whether he could give up the not inconsiderable time next year which the preliminary trial races, followed by the series itself, would take if we were to be selected. At 34 ft overall, *Morning Cloud* was too small to be eligible for the team (which has to be made up of boats within certain sizes, the dimensions of which vary occasionally, but which are generally fairly large), so it was obvious that we would have to have a new boat.

The first *Cloud* had been a production boat with a fibreglass hull and deck of a standard Sparkman & Stephens design – the so-called S&S 34. This time it was decided that we would have a one-off boat specially designed, and built in wood. I know that Mr Heath would have preferred to go to a British designer for this commission, but two factors weighed heavily against this. First, at that time the Stephens brothers were by far the most successful designers for the type of boat he had in mind, standing head and shoulders clear of anyone else. Secondly, he had formed a close working relationship with Olin Stephens following the purchase of the first *Morning Cloud* from Mike Winfield. Their first meeting on the Winfield stand at the London Boat Show was one of those encounters where fate might or might not have been given a helping hand. To all intents and purposes it was pure chance that Olin was on the stand where the S&S 34 was being displayed when Mr Heath came along to see the boat again, after a previous tour of the Show when he had been round the entire hall. Few people knew that he was to make a return visit, but Mike Winfield was certainly one of them, though he probably did not know the exact time. Now, Olin Stephens was not the sort of man to hang around all day waiting for a meeting, so we can certainly give Dame Fortune some, if not all, of the credit for the happy coincidence. At all events, from this encounter grew an excellent business association, which was fostered as we got the boat ready for the Southern Cross series in Australia, when Olin was of particular help in advising on modifications to take advantage of the rule by putting stringers round the inside of the hull.

So it was decided quite early in 1970 that we would go to Sparkman & Stephens for the design, and that she would be built in wood. There was a lot of sense in choosing a builder on the south coast, because a number of the crew lived in the area and would be able to watch her progress. Moodys, Camper & Nicholson and Lallows were all obvious candidates and Mr Heath finally chose Lallows in Cowes, partly because it was hoped that Ian Lallow, Clare's son, might be able to sail with us. I've got a funny feeling that it was me who first suggested Lallows for the job but, as usual, the whole crew had a say and Mr Heath then made the final choice.

Meanwhile *Morning Cloud* returned from her triumph on the other side of the world, and I went to Dunkirk to sail her back to the Hamble River. This proved to be a minor epic in itself. First, the mast had been lashed on deck for the trip, so I had to arrange for it to be stepped. The rigging was stowed properly, because we had done this ourselves in Tasmania, but there was no dockside crane which could do the job, so I had to set about hiring one. French is not my strong point, and I was mentally exhausted by the time the whole thing was over and done with. Then the weather took a hand. The temperature dropped and the wind went firmly into the west, so we had a beat for the whole trip, which must have established some sort of record for the longest ever Dunkirk–Solent. When we got home we were frozen stiff and I remember thinking 'If this is sailing, I'll give it up for good.'

We got her ready for the 1970 season, which was spent carefully observing every other successful boat we encountered. Each man was to have his say in the layout of the new boat, so we all determined to be in a position to know what was the latest thinking as regards our own particular area.

Once again, although Mr Heath was paying for the new boat, we all looked on her as ours. She was, in fact, more 'our' boat than any I have ever sailed in, because we all put so much thought into her. As I have said, we looked at every other boat from a new angle, because we wanted to get the new one right. In the end, we virtually designed the deck layout ourselves, to the outline plan which Olin and Rod Stephens drew for us. The foredeck men said how they wanted the gear arranged up front, this was dovetailed into the requirements of the cockpit crew, providing it all fitted in with the midship hands. We had a lot of fun planning it all, and Mr Heath went along with virtually everything we suggested. This was done at more breakfast meetings, this time at 10 Downing Street or Chequers, the Prime Minister's official country home. There was a harmony among us all from the word go; we were excited and, from the first, felt that we were helping to organise a winner.

We knew, of course, that some pretty hot competition was being prepared in other camps, so selection for the team was by no means a foregone conclusion. We should have to prove by racing our brainchild that we had not only got a good hull and efficient layout, but that we could turn in the results. All this kept us keyed up to a high pitch as 1970 passed by. The boat was due to be laid down in October, and Olin and Rod Stephens were marvellous in the way they took our suggestions and turned them into working plans; sometimes, of course, they had to tell us that we could not have what we were asking, but they always came up with a good alternative. For instance, Anthony Churchill obviously had his ideas on how he wanted the navigation area laid out. These were put to the designers, who said whether it could be done or made suggestions for minor changes. Everything went forward happily and without a hitch, so that Lallows had the plans in plenty of time to start work at the beginning of the winter. And I was able to cross over to Cowes at any time to help iron out snags, but there were remarkably few.

The final layout of the boat was fairly radical by the standards of the day. We had taken the winches off the mast and mounted them on deck. It sounds ridiculous now to have to go on your knees to wind a winch, without benefit of a well cockpit, but this was all to reduce windage on the mast. The spinnaker pole lifts and downhauls were all led aft to the cockpit. Our hatches were sliding, rather than up-and-over, to make it easier to pass sails through them (though we never really managed to make them water tight), and we had a seastay with a (single) luff groove for the genoa. We had a trim tab on the keel, copied from the twelves and not penalised by the rule in those days, and steering was by tiller.

Launching was in the spring of 1971, and from the first it was obvious that the boat was a flyer. She was what I call a forgiving boat, always ready to make amends for mistakes on the part of the crew. If you got a bad start it was almost as if she were saying 'So you made a mess of it. All right, I'll get you out of it.' And away she'd go, working her way to windward, passing other boats through their lee if necessary, until she got a clean wind.

Selection

We won practically everything we tried our hands at, so it was evident early on that we would be in the team. Another boat to do well was Arthur Slater's new *Prospect of Whitby*, who came good fairly soon after they had added some weight to her keel; Ian Lallow was sailing in her, as was my old mate from the *Kurrewa* days, Wally Smythers. The third boat was not so easy to choose, for there was a wealth of talent competing for the honour, among them a new *Noryema* for Ron Amey, Donald Parr's *Quailo* which was one of the new Nicholson 55's, and finally *Cervantes IV*, another Sparkman & Stephens design of about our size. The third place boiled down to a fight between these last two in the end, and finally Bob Watson's *Cervantes* got the nod.

Then, to cap our pleasure at being selected, the RORC announced that Mr Heath was to be team captain. He, of course, was as delighted as we were, and entered into his duties with gusto. Being the man he is, he can quickly weld a team together – he had proved that to us in Australia, was doing it as Prime Minister, and now soon had everybody in the three British boats determined to win honours for their country. The competition was very hot, and some really lovely boats were to be seen sailing in UK waters, as the fleet gathered together and indulged in the early warm-up races. *Morning Cloud* was a yacht to be really proud of. She was also the one they all wanted to see. Moored opposite the Groves and Gutteridge marina at Cowes, we were continually being asked if we would show people over her, and it made you feel good to know that it was our boat which everybody thought was the best laid out and equipped – and she was never more 'ours' than at those moments. We had put a lot of effort and time into perfecting her, and we might have been forgiven if we allowed our pride in her pre-eminent position to show. There was not another yacht to touch her, and the Japanese, who were just then entering serious racing for the first time, were particularly attentive with their cameras and gesticulations.

Mr Heath's translation to the top office in the land caused quite a stir in sailing circles, as you may imagine. The crew of *Morning Cloud* liked to think (quite incorrectly, I am sure) that they had helped in a small way to put him into 10 Downing Street. By winning the Sydney–Hobart race he had shown himself to be not only an able politician and statesman, but also a hard racing skipper, able to take all that the elements offered and come out on top of an international field; his personality blossomed to a new dimension in the light of the nationwide acclaim which he received.

But it also brought its problems. The security people started fussing around, and made all sorts of impractical suggestions; then the political pundits had to have their say regarding access, should the Skipper be needed on the helm at Westminster while he was steering his boat in an offshore race. We had to find room for a lot of heavy radio gear, and arrangements were proposed for lifting him off by helicopter if need arose. We didn't like the turn the plans were taking.

'What happens to *Morning Cloud* while all this is going on, sir?' I asked, speaking for us all and fearing the worst.

'Oh, she'll have to heave-to and lower her sails until it's all over,' was the reply from the Whitehall spokesman.

'To hell with that.' I knew I was voicing the opinion of the crew, but was equally aware that Mr Heath was also listening. 'We race to win and we don't stop for anybody, Prime Minister or no Prime Minister. If you want him, we'll put him over the side in a rubber dinghy and you can come and fetch him.'

'Excellent, excellent,' laughed Mr Heath, to my considerable relief as he turned to his advisers. 'That's the spirit I like to hear. You see gentlemen, you have your answer.'

The Series

And so it was arranged. Fortunately we never had to do it, so I was not called upon to cast a Prime Minister adrift on the open sea. He arranged his programme very well, and there were not a lot of races he had to miss. He planned to sail all the Admiral's Cup races, including the Fastnet and, though we seemed to be somewhat below our previous high standard, we did well enough to win the trophy. The team had a good Channel race, because *Prospect* won, we were third and *Cervantes* fourth, so we were off to a good points start. The first inshore race was a disappointment, for *Cervantes* was disqualified, but *Prospect* was second and we were fourth. This was a race which Mr Heath had to miss because he was kept in the House of Commons at the last minute. The Americans and Australians were now hard on our heels.

The *Cloud* then had a poorish tenth in the second inshore race, when we never seemed to get it together, and the Australians moved even closer. We had had a wonderful build-up, but then were unwise enough to take a month's lay off because we feared that we might become stale. As it happened, we went off the boil and never got back to our original form, so the actual racing was a bit of a let down. We have never let this happen in subsequent *Morning Clouds*. I think we unconsciously felt that the boat would lift us out of trouble as she had done before, but we were in a hot league now and couldn't afford any lapses. Then in the high-scoring Fastnet race we carried away the track for the spinnaker pole on the fore side of the mast, which meant lashing the pole to the mast, with attendant problems every time we had to gybe. I don't offer this as an excuse, but we didn't do too well – it's funny, but none of the *Clouds* has ever had a good Fastnet. We didn't let the team down, because although Syd Fischer's *Ragamuffin* won that particular race for Australia, their team's chances were ruined when *Koomooloo* carried away her rudder. *Cervantes* made up for her earlier disqualification by coming third overall, and *Prospect* had a fairly good result.

It was enough to win the Admiral's Cup for Britain. We were all particularly pleased, because the Skipper was Prime Minister, and it can't have been easy for him to organise his time so that he could play a full part as team captain. In the middle of the series racing we had also collected the Gold Roman Bowl as overall winner of the Round the Island race for the third successive year – a feat never before or since achieved by one owner. The feeling of success and resulting jubilation remain with me to this day as one of the high spots of my career.

If the second *Cloud* had one failing, it was that she would never get above 8½ knots down wind. Other boats would surf down a wave at a speed well above their theoretical maximum, but not us. We tried everything, from altering the rake to shifting weight; we even had crew members running forward as we dipped into a trough on the back of a wave and then doubling aft as we reached the bottom. I came to the conclusion that we would never do it, probably through some quirk of hull shape and immersed volume.

Although it was a broach which carried away our spinnaker pole tracks on the Fastnet, the boat did not display the unpleasant down wind habits of some fin and skeg designs, and she was pretty well mannered on the whole. We did have enough hard work on the tiller coming back from the Rock, with a 40 knot wind behind us, however, to make us decide to change to wheel steering for the 1972 season.

Above all, we were a happy ship. Mr Heath made an easy going skipper who could tolerate the odd mistake without undue displeasure, but woe betide the habitual offender! I have a pretty even temper myself, and got along with the Skipper very well. I recall one occasion, however, when he became rather repetitive about some point, so that I felt that we had heard enough.

'You are going on a bit,' I ventured. 'You're not in the House of Commons now, you know.'

We fed well on offshore races in all the *Clouds*. When the Skipper became Prime Minister, he had food specially prepared at Chequers and sent down, each dish labelled: Meal 1, Meal 2 and so on. The first race like this produced roast duckling with orange sauce, and fillet steaks with all the trimmings, so that we fed like lords – better I suspect, for I'd wager that the House of Lords Yacht Club never fared so well. We were then told to put it to the vote, and decided against this rather rich fare and asked whether we could have casseroles, stews, steaks (one of the easiest meals both to cook and to eat when you are standing on your ear), with plenty of soups. Similarly, we had been asked in the first *Morning Cloud* whether we wanted cans of beer on board, but we had voted for a 'dry' ship, going for colas, squash and the odd shandy which is always thirst quenching; I believe that there was half a bottle of medicinal brandy on board, but we never had cause to open it.

The crew took it in turns to heat the meals, but I must confess that I often found something else to do when it came to cooking anything other than a pot of tea; perhaps the shades of my early encounter with the paraffin stove on *Clover* were still haunting me. Then there has always been a hard tack box, with biscuits, chocolate wafers and boiled sweets for the night watch, or anyone else who was hungry between meals. We sail hard, we eat well and we leave the celebrating until we get ashore when, as I have already said, we go round together as a crew, Skipper included.

Tailpiece

The Black Deck

Owen Torrey

This piece was written by Owen Torrey, of Charles Ulmer Sailmakers Inc. It first appeared in 1973 in the American magazine Yacht Racing for the One Design and Offshore Yachtsman, *now called* Yacht Racing/Cruising. *It is unparalleled as an affectionate and detailed satire on the contemporary American offshore racing scene.*

It all started when the girl in the office at Derecktor's got confused filling out a work order for Bus Mosbacher's new One Ton boat. It was supposed to have black topsides and a white deck and somehow or other things got transposed. Anyhow, the boat came out with white topsides and a black deck. Bus was pretty upset because everybody knows that a boat with a black deck can get pretty hot and uncomfortable in the summertime, but there wasn't time enough before the One Ton Regatta at Newport to do anything about it. The boat was late already. So Bus took it to Newport the way it was.

It was pretty grim going because the weather was uncommonly hot and the temperature in the cabin hovered around 120 degrees. It wasn't much better on deck either, especially if you tried to sit down.

Being the fine unflappable sailor that he is, Bus nevertheless managed to win the series, which had attracted rather more than the usual coverage by the press. I guess that's what led to some of the trouble because there were a lot of reporters on the dock after the last race trying for interviews. One in particular, a very pretty non-sailor from *The Christian Science Monitor*, was especially insistent. Bus answered her many questions with his usual graciousness, but the ordeal of sailing five or six long races in an oven had worn him down a little. Inevitably, he was asked what single thing was most responsible for his victory. He replied, just a little brusquely perhaps, that it was obviously the black deck, and in due course it all appeared that way in the press.

A lot of people wondered why a black deck would make a boat go any faster, but it wasn't long before a number of them appeared on the race courses around the country. Speculation continued as to the merits of the black deck, and in due course a number of technical articles on the subject appeared in the yachting magazines. One of the most widely read of these was by a technical writer in a popular sailboat monthly who explained at considerable length that the warm air rising from the deck would inhibit the flow of wind around the underside of the mainsail from the windward side to the leeward side. This was characterised as an 'Induced Collateral End Plate' which served to double the effective aspect ratio of the rig. There must have been some merit in the argument for very soon more black decks appeared around the country.

Unfortunately, these were no more comfortable than Mosbacher's had been. Some people even began to wonder whether the extra speed attributed to the black deck was worth the discomfort. Luckily, at this point a number of marine suppliers, especially West Products, came out with some partial remedies for the problem. A new super light insulating material was developed with which to line the overhead. It was sort of unsightly and a little expensive to install but there is no doubt that it helped. On deck the problem was eased by specially insulated Topsiders and racing shorts with insulation in the seat.

By this time, there were enough black decks in evidence so that the International Technical Committee of the IOR decided to make a study. Pending the results of their investigation, it was decided to assess an arbitrary 0·75 per cent penalty on the rating of any boat with a black deck. Not to be outdone, the Storm Trysail Club concluded that the ITC's penalty was probably wrong and assessed one of their own which was 0·875 per cent. When these penalties were announced, a number of owners who had previously been on the fence concluded that there must indeed be some merit in the black deck, and so quite a few more appeared in the various racing fleets.

Naturally, the matter came to be referred to the various naval architects for opinions. The most complete reply, in terms of words per unit of message, came from S & S who put out a document which might be called a 'White Paper on Black Decks'. It ran on for several very well written pages and concluded with the observation that although any number of colours might be selected for the purpose of painting a deck, black was certainly the darkest, at least so far as that term is commonly understood.

By this time, a number of variations on the theme of 'Basic Black' appeared. After it was learned that the report that Hard Sails had obtained a patent on plain back paint was proven to be untrue, most people followed the obvious course and used it. A few followed more esoteric routes, however. For example, Jessie Phillips had a special mixture prepared for *Charisma*, in which pulverized titanium was used as the pigment. This was of course a lot more expensive, but it was somewhat lighter and became generally known as 'Light Black'. Dr Jerome Milgram, former Thistle sailor, stole a march on the fleet by using midnight blue instead of black, thus avoiding the rating penalty. This took the ITC by surprise and they began to investigate the possibilities of using a light meter to measure the reflectance of the surface, regardless of colour. Meanwhile, pending the results of this investigation, an arbitrary 10 per cent rating penalty was assessed against Professor Milgram's boat. The incident served among other things to increase the newspaper interview value of that boat from $50,000 to $67,000.

Another clever variation was conceived by Britton Chance for Jack Potter's *Equation*. It was found that whatever the merits of a black deck might be in the sunlight, these did not apply at night, and there were, at night at least, some disadvantages. Accordingly, Britt designed a deck which consisted of a series of louvres, somewhat reminiscent of venetian blind panels running athwartships. These were painted black on one side and white on the other and by the simple operation of a hydraulic control, they could be isolated so as to expose either the white side or the black side. The arrangement worked beautifully and the pumps were easily able to keep up with the leaks.

By the time the next year's Bermuda Race rolled around, virtually the entire fleet was equipped with black decks. Unfortunately, it was a very slow, long and hot race. Even with the specially insulated and air conditioned boats and the special clothing, many of the crews became so exhausted that they were forced to withdraw when the wind died as they neared Bermuda. Surprisingly enough, the race was won by Bus Mosbacher who, unlike his competitors, was as fresh as a daisy when he stepped ashore. It seems that after considerable argument with Derecktor, he had finally succeeded in having the error rectified and his deck painted white. Bus had little to say about his victory except a casual remark to the effect that 'We just kept her moving all the time.'

Mast Failure
Photographer Janet Harber writes: These two pictures were taken at the 1968 Burnham Icicle Race. I was working from the shore using a telephoto lens, near the start-line at the Royal Corinthian. It was a particularly windy Icicle – a near gale, if I remember, and the dinghies were reaching back and forth across the river before the start. The Enterprise was all lined up in my viewfinder and I was about to press the shutter to record what I thought would be a dinghy at full chat when the mast buckled in front of my eyes. The camera shake is because I couldn't believe what I was seeing!

Cruising: Two Philosophies

Sailing by Eye

J D Sleightholme
Cruising
first published 1963

Originally published as Pocket Cruising, *J D Sleightholme's book is now titled simply* Cruising, *and is already in the second printing of its third edition. He introduces the following extract with these words: 'I have always believed that to con a boat by eye alone has great merit in that one assembles a sort of mental chart and a "feeling of position" on it. The headlands, buoys, marks and landmarks wheel around you as you pass by, offering a constant mental plot of changing position.*

'I think I would add one important point to the following extract; con by eye for all you are worth, but from time to time, as positions on the chart present themselves, mark them as such with the time and the heading. If you are running the log, note that also. Then if suddenly your eyebrows go up and your confidence goes down – if you are momentarily lost or caught out by failing visibility – you have a last known position from which to plot.'

There is nothing frighteningly technical about the sort of navigation, or coastal pilotage to give it a more exact name, required for small cruisers. The simpler it can be made the better. Without the big chart-table and steadier working surface on bigger craft, the small boat man will get on better by sticking to a very few rules than by trying to work to fine limits.

The ancient Norse pilots worked by studying headlands. They had no instruments, but they had a keen eye for the shape of the land. The pocket-cruiser man has the advantages of charts, compasses and tide-tables, but he is attempting much the same type of navigation.

Above all things he must be a map reader. This is no heresy, and it does not mean that he should use a map in lieu of a chart. But he will have very little time in which to practise chart work at sea, and map-reading from a one-inch Ordnance Survey before he goes will teach him to look at the flat sheet and visualise it as a landscape or coastline which has height and depth.

Most navigational trouble arises from losing one's sense of orientation. One can get lost while in full view of a clearly recognisable stretch of coastline, merely because one has failed to 'look' at the coast in the bustle of laying courses, reading logs and taking innumerable bearings on buoys. It needs but one or two of these fixes to go wrong and one begins to get anxious. So the first thing to do in a small coasting cruiser is to keep a constant watch on the coastline as it unfolds, at the same time studying the chart.

Plotting is often a labour in a bit of a sea. Watching the coast calls for no instruments, and fixes upon buoys and shore-marks are only for confirmation. The compass course may be used when there is risk of suddenly losing visibility or it may be a simple matter of convenience for steering straight. At other times it is really only important if there are offlying dangers athwart the course, which have to be given a known safe berth, or in verifying a transit when there is doubt about the identification of one of the objects.

It is possible to navigate clear along a coastline without looking at the instruments, simply by noting the natural transits provided by headlands, piers, rocks and so on. By laying a ruler on the chart, for instance, the yachtsman may notice a headland which, at a certain point, becomes obscured behind a bulge in the coast. By watching for it he gets a position line which is indisputable and, if at the same time, a glance ashore shows a small bay or group of rocks coming abeam he has his second line – rough, of course, but a succession of such transit fixes takes him safely down the coast without him once becoming involved in the complexity of chart work which seems to be considered so vital.

I mention this habit of studying the coast first for an important reason. There are times when a man has his hands far too full sailing the boat to indulge in lengthy sessions on the chart. If he can 'see' his way along it will stand him in good stead. But first he must learn to see the coast as a chart and the chart as a coast. This chapter deals with pilotage by eye and the look of the land from seaward. In the next chapter the use of compass, calculation of tidal effect, laying a course offshore and so on will be dealt with stage by stage.

Looking at the Land

Each coastal region has its own typical features. The East Coast man is often terrified of West Coast rockiness and the deep-water man, accustomed to rock-fringed coasts, is nervous of navigating among the shallows of the Thames Estuary. Nowadays the owner of a small cruiser may trail it from one coast to the other in the course of a day, and so he must be a versatile navigator.

The low-lying coastline is particularly difficult to identify. The shape of the sea-bed usually continues the run of the flat shore, and it is therefore shallow for a long way out to sea. This means that the cruiser is forced to stay well out, and details on shore become harder to identify. The absence

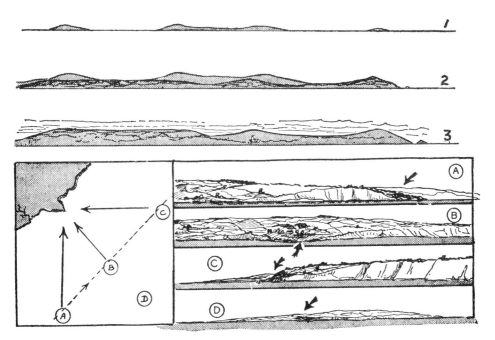

Fig. 36 Approaching the coast in clear visibility, distant hills may be seen in a row of islands (1). Nearer inshore (2) the foreground is still overshadowed by the inland contour, but close inshore the inland hills are hidden and the skyline shape of the coast is quite changed (3). The small headland seen from positions A, B and C may be hard to distinguish against the rest of the coastline although from the chart it would promise to be easily identified. At position D, well offshore, only a slight sharpening of detail indicates its position.

of pronounced headlands, cliffs, distinctive bays and rocky outcrops complicates things further. Headlands run out to sea so gradually that the exact point where the land finishes and sea begins is hard to decide. On this kind of coast the navigator becomes a buoy-hopper. He concentrates entirely on buoys and ignores the land, and he can easily lose his sense of position if he makes a mistake in a compass course between buoys.

The low coastline rises and falls in hazy undulations and it's difficult to decide whether a gradual fading away into the sea is due to the height of the land diminishing or the coastline receding. The only clues are such objects as houses, trees and people ashore. Compare them constantly through the binoculars and note their relative sizes at different spots along the coastline.

The direction of natural light must be reckoned with. If the sun is low and behind the land there will be a featureless monotony of bluish shadow in which a block of flats may look no different from a church-tower, or a clump of trees may masquerade as a prominent spur of ground shown on the chart. On the other hand the sunlight shining full onshore can pick out a strip of wet road and make it appear to be a white tower, while the actual tower is muted by the shadow of a cloud. You must therefore never accept the obvious without due thought.

A hilly coast is far easier to correlate to the chart. The yacht is usually close inshore and bays and headlands are more distinct, also villages and small towns do not straggle, each is contained more compactly in its valley. There is only the risk of one headland looking much like another, especially with the effect of sunshine and cloud shadow to alter the apparent contours.

Seen from far at sea the contours of a coastline can be very deceptive if there are ranges of inland hills. The switchback effect of more distant hills may be quite different from the actual coastline profile, and only as the yacht gets closer are the background hills hidden by the coastline. It must

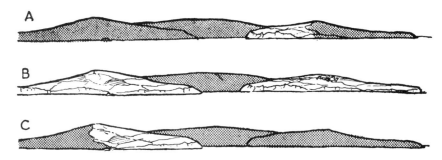

Fig. 37 Sunlight striking a hilly coast can alter the importance of prominent features. 'A' highlights the right-hand headland, but 'B' gives an impression of a deep inlet, while 'C' from a distance might cause the right-hand headland to look like a receding coastline.

be remembered that bays and headlands seen from offshore are fore-shortened. Often it is only low-slanting sunlight, casting shadow, which reveals the position of a headland at all. The navigator may sail straight past it only to find it, as he thinks, some miles further on when a lesser headland is exaggerated by tricks of light (Fig. 37).

It is easy to con a cruiser by identifying prominent features as they come into line ashore once you have mastered the symbols on the chart and learnt to match land and paper in this way. In tricky waters, infested with rocks or sand-bars, it is no substitute for careful plotting with compass and parallel rules, but it dispenses with 80 per cent of it in straightforward waters, while the safe transit method of keeping an offing from inshore dangers is better than any mechanical plot.

Many transits (objects in line) are marked on the chart for the guidance of the navigator approaching a river or passage between dangers, and most of these are man-made beacons, towers and so forth. The coastline furnishes many, many more which are there for the finding.

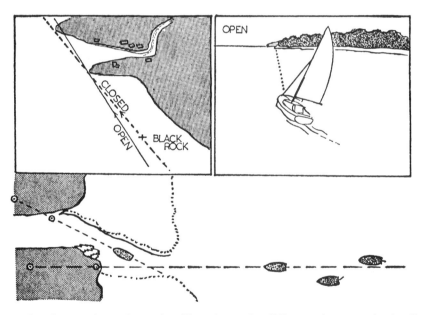

Fig. 38 Leading marks and transits. Plan shows the difference between the headlands 'closed', or the nearer one covering the more distant headland, and 'open', when the distant headland can be seen projecting beyond the nearer one. In this case the headlands are being kept open as an indication that the cruiser is clearing Black Rock which lies on the transit of the headlands. Leading marks (bottom) may be man-made beacons for entering a river, the vessel steering to keep the back mark in line with the front one. In this case there are two sets of leaders, an inner pair guiding the vessel into the river. The leaders may be lit by night.

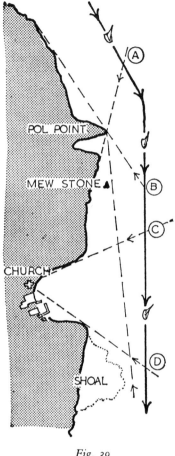

Fig. 39

In Fig. 39 the cruiser is coasting offshore along the unbroken arrowed line. At 'A' headlands are in transit, and at 'B' a headland hides the bulge in the coastline astern. Yet another transit of sorts comes up as the bay opens up from 'C', and at 'D' the navigator finds a safe transit to see him past the shoal. By glancing at the church-tower he knows that he will not be in the danger area until it is lost to view behind the land, while by keeping the Mew Stone astern *inside* Pol point he can stay outside the danger area.

There will be buoys to aid him, naturally, but it isn't always so easy for the inexperienced navigator to be certain of the identity of a buoy until he is close. The buoy which appears where he would *like* to see it may not be the one he is hoping to find, and, of course, there is no excuse for not checking the compass bearings between buoys as they are passed. Many of them form useful transits in their own right, but it must be borne in mind that at close hand the swinging room of a moored buoy upsets the angles a lot, especially if it should be a little out of position. Both buoys and light-ships rarely get out of position, but occasionally they do so and they ought not to be relied upon implicitly.

The chart usually gives a picture of compactness with the buoys in cosy proximity to each other. In reality the details are unexpectedly distant, and the whole picture greatly extended. An observer takes in the whole chart-coast at a glance, but the land is seen as a mass which tapers in perspective on either hand. The buoys marked on the chart would need to be engraved as pin-pricks to approximate to their correct scale, and it is important to think of them as pin-pricks. At a distance of three miles a really large buoy

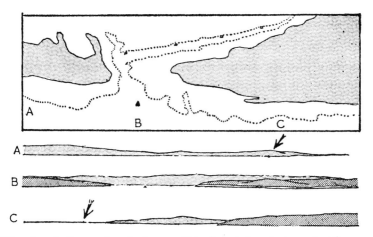

Fig. 40 The chart indicates that the buoy will be found close inshore, but from positions A and C it may be missed, since it will appear to be lost against the background in the one case and further offshore in the other. At B it becomes plain to find if the yacht has made a proper approach.

can just about be seen, though probably not identified, and the smaller buoys without topmarks are not visible until within one and a half miles. The navigator studying his chart may expect to see half a dozen buoys all within a small area and he may get worried because they don't show up. In coasting, it is a common mistake to look too close inshore for an expected buoy probably marking an offlying spit. In fact, it may be visible as a tiny black peppercorn apparently far out to sea. But once you reach it, the coastline behind it appears close again due to the effect of foreshortening. Practice with the ordinary Ordnance Survey map ashore helps a lot by giving you a feeling of distance away from land. Coasting and keeping a safe distance offshore are largely a matter of judgement. The navigator may cover his chart with fixes, but when the shore is featureless and barren of seamarks it is judgement which counts.

Distance by Eye

It is deceptive to attempt to judge distance through binoculars. Distance blurs detail even though the object may be visible for a long way. A large tree at between one and a half and two miles can be seen in crisp detail in a good light, but if a pencil is held at arm's length, the tree will be no taller than the lead. At four miles the tree is seen with rounded outlines, and shadows are blue, with the foliage masses appearing to have been dabbed on roughly, though the shapes of trees are still quite individual. At eight miles trees are simply blue humps and can easily be confused with, say, a water tower or a row of houses.

A small building with a white or pale facing wall becomes blurred and loses sharp edges at a mile and a half although darker windows and doors are still recognisable. At four miles these details have gone and the shape is almost lost. At six miles it has become a dab of colour without shape. Caravan parks at five miles are scattered chips of white, cars can be seen if they are moving and hedgerows are about the size of a pencil line.

The effect of lighting is again very important. A coastline under the full blaze of early morning sunshine is crisp in detail and appears closer than it does with the detail lost in shadow. At dusk, with the light behind the land making it a flat silhouette and the reflection of high ground extending across the water, it is often hard to form any true estimate. This is especially true at night and many a cruiser has navigated inshore to find an anchorage, and finally anchored at what seems to be a perilously close distance from the shore; but daylight finds her stuck out in the open a mile from land. The black land mass and its reflection seem to loom far higher than it really is.

Weather also affects one's judgement of distance. The vivid clarity which often comes in advance of rain and wind can mess up the estimates; the pearly haze of a hot day, which so often accompanies easterly weather, or the refraction which seems to jack up the whole coastline, must all be reckoned with. Refraction, extending the height of shore buildings to a grotesque proportion, can fool the navigator into thinking that a row of particularly nasty bungalows are actually oil storage tanks. The beach also becomes a prominent feature, to be searched for anxiously on the chart, though it is really just a narrow strip of shingle.

The effect of the earth's curvature when one is looking for shoremarks also comes into the picture when visibility is very clear. A harbour wall, sole clue to a small port perhaps, may be 'dipped' just below the horizon when the town behind it is vividly seen in detail, and at night whole rows of shore lights can be seen jauntily nipping up and down with a disturbing ripple effect.

The Look of the Water

Without a certain knowledge of position, a passage down the coast becomes rather frightening. Every wind ripple or tidal swirl becomes, in the imagination, an 'uncharted' rock. The look of the water is a necessary study.

In rocky coastal districts the colour of the water is significant. Blue-black for the deeps, paler blue and then green for shoal patches, with black shadows marking underwater rocks covered with weed – in sunshine the pilot can get plenty of warning of shoaling water. On the east coast of England, however, it is rare to find clear water, and a two-foot patch is often the same colour as a ten-fathom channel. In fact the swirl of a fast tide may bring sand to the surface and imitate a shoal where none exists. The movement of the water is another matter altogether.

In Fig. 41 some of the many faces of the sea are shown. At 'A' unbalanced breaking crests give warning of rocks beneath. This is familiar deep-water rocky coast stuff and there may be ample water above the rocks, but they must still be avoided. The sheen on the water above a sandbank 'B' is often imitated by a 'hole' in the wind on a quiet day, but with the least breeze there will be a subtle change in the surface of the water which is unmistakable. 'C' shows how a tidal overfall may look very similar to a shoal or reef. At 'D' a calm sea allows the tidal stream running through the deeper water of the channel to reveal its whereabouts by a rippling of the surface. Note how the awash shoal by the beacon is barely distinguishable from the water around it. The same channel in a light breeze 'E' may be marked by a slick of smooth water if the stream is flowing, with the wind, fast enough to prevent the formation of wavelets. At 'F', however, wind against tide has raised a steep sea in the deep water, while the regular wave-formation indicates shallower water where the fast tide is not felt. 'G' shows the same channel when the stream is running with the wind and the higher waves are seen over the shallower water. Open-sea waves of a trochoidal type of swell (H) may be left-overs from a distant storm, they may be high but they are usually harmless. In shoaling water the crests may spill forward, and again not necessarily be troublesome. The cycloidal wind-driven wave, which increases in size according to 'fetch' or distance unimpeded by land, frequently becomes a plunger in shoal water and must be avoided. The shallow bar 'I' seen from seaward is deceptive because only the backs of the breaking waves are seen. Overfalls are often caused by an abrupt rise in the sea-bed 'J' which forces the tidal current on the surface, but an isolated rocky outcrop may also be the cause. It is dangerous to venture close to any overfall unless the exact depth of water is known. To skirt it in order to stay on a making tack, for instance, is risky since the actual water disturbance takes place at various distances from the rock itself. A fast tide in deep water creates 'smooths' or slicks which may be frightening, suggesting as they do some unseen rock 'K'. The yacht may

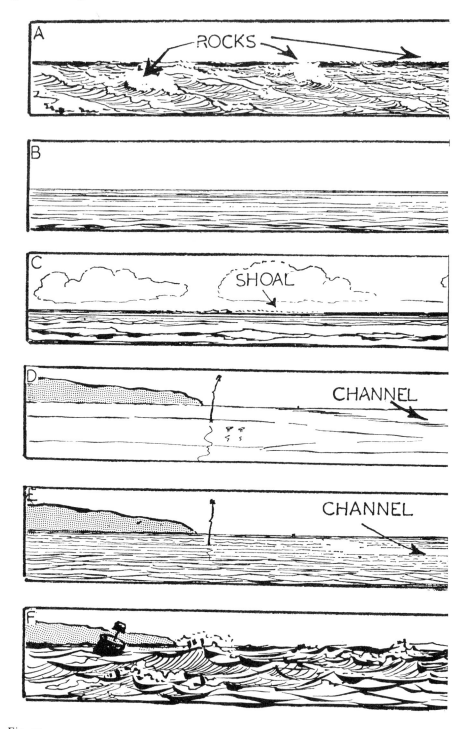

Fig. 41

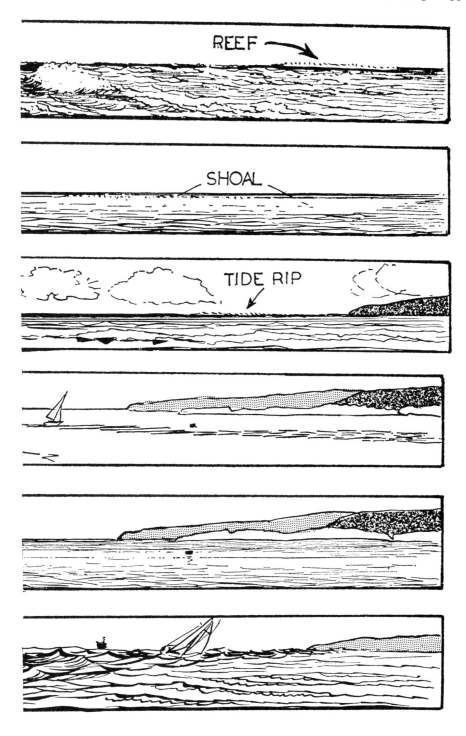

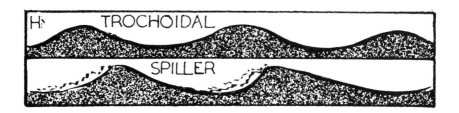

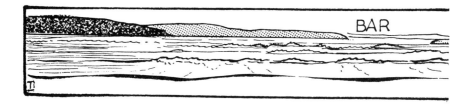

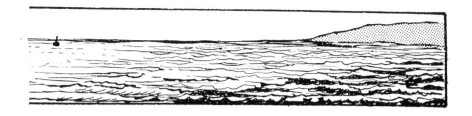

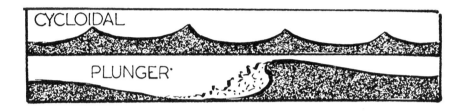

CYCLOIDAL

PLUNGER·

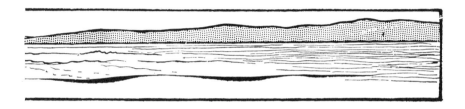

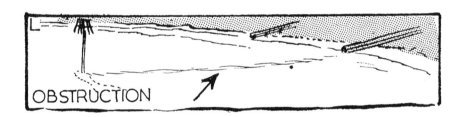

L

OBSTRUCTION

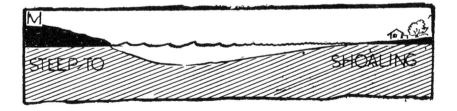

M

STEEP TO　　　　　　　SHOALING

be spun completely around in a slick, but the real danger comes if there is a sea running, when a 'race' may develop which can overpower a small boat. The ripple above an underwater obstruction 'L' is a good guide close inshore when the outer mark may have passed unnoticed further out to seaward. At 'M' is a section of shore showing the difference between shoal and steep-to coasts. Note how the diminishing size of wave in shallow water, due to the slacker tidal stream, is a guide to the nature of the bottom.

Galley Equipment

Bob Heppel
Seacook: A Guide to Good Living Afloat
first published 1979

Bob Heppel's varied sailing career helps to make his book on cooking in small boats a colourful addition to the list. He writes:

'*As a small boy I was addicted to sea tales: my heroes were all admirals, and I read avidly of their great voyages. I remember being horrified not so much by the brutality of life at sea, nor by the appalling living conditions afloat, but by the nauseating diet which caused repulsive diseases and a painful death for 90 per cent of the crews. At the age of twelve, when sailing my very first boat, I resolved that though I might be drowned, could well be wrecked, would surely have to endure physical discomfort when voyaging, I would take great care never to suffer a slow, painful death from malnutrition.*

'*As a teenager, on holiday with friends who were professional fishermen working out of Newlyn, I was invited to join as deckhand in lobster-potting along the coast to Lamorna. I shall never forget the disgusting brew of hot liquid, tasting of soot, paraffin, tea leaves, condensed milk and too much sugar served in a chipped, stained enamel mug too hot to hold; nor the revulsion at the sight of a cornish pasty taken from a rusty, leaking biscuit tin and doled out by hands well grimed with fish scales, engine grease, diesel fuel and blood from fish hook wounds and lobster nips; nor the incongruity of using a small, handleless leaky bucket as a loo, with the whole of the western approaches before me; but I was never seasick.*

'*Experience steeled my resolve never to sail without the wherewithal to cook and keep clean. The equipment for this would be as efficient and functional as my sails, my gear and my engine. I would have a planned galley and clean heads. All this began so many years ago that I have long lived in comfort and ease as I sail. Time now allows me to regard the average café cook as a destroyer of food, restaurateurs as rogues and yachtsmen who pay to eat ashore as fools.'*

The Stove

First and foremost among the inducements needed to encourage a good cook must come a good stove. Certain minimum requirements can be set out for any cooker used afloat. First the stove top should be large enough to take a quart-sized saucepan or a pressure cooker together with a normal-sized frying pan, at one and the same time. A top on which it is possible to heat a large kettle or a frying pan, but not both together is severely restricted. Remember always that, unlike the caravan, a boat is not surrounded by miles of terra firma upon which to light auxiliary fires or to set up extra burners for more pots and pans. There is the space of the galley and no more, for it has long been forbidden to walk on the water. Before you believe the stove to be large enough, therefore, arm yourself with a rectangle of card upon which your pressure cooker and frying pan fit; this is the pattern. Don't be distracted with suggestions that there are smaller pots and smaller pans. They do a smaller job – and who wants smaller meals after a day's sailing?

Ideally the stove should have at least two burners and a grill. The grill pan must be large enough to take four pork chops and the distance between chops and the burner must be sufficient to prevent the flames licking the chops before you do. To test for size take a large nautical almanac and put it beneath the grill in the pan. It may be felt that an oven is also a necessity. Roasting and baking are time-consuming processes, usually measured in hours, and time is at a premium while enjoyably sailing. With the exception of bread and pastry, most roasting dishes can be pot-roasted in the pressure cooker in a much shorter period. If, however, it is resolved to install an oven, make sure that the oven door may be opened and the inside examined without crouching in the loo or slipping a disc under the cabin table. Check the size of the oven: an adult shoe box is a good approximation. Envisage a chicken for four replacing the shoe box and do not allow your suspicion that the oven is too small to be lulled by suggestions that re-heated chicken pies are an alternative to a roasted bird. Reject the small oven. If asbestos mats are used on the top burners, a covered baking dish will enable the pies to be warmed. An oven is not then necessary.

The stove must have a fiddle rail around the four sides. These rails must not prevent the frying pan from sitting flat on the stove top. Some stove fiddle rails are so high that the projecting pan handle rests on the rail, thus preventing the pan from lying flat on the burner. A pair of adjustable locking bars should be fitted to the rails so that pots may be rigidly fixed; a substitute for such locking devices may be made from wire. If a ring is formed which will fit the exterior of the saucepan or pot, and from the ring a hook is contrived which will catch over the fiddle rail, the pot will be securely anchored.

Finally, as they say in the world of cooking afloat, 'to gimbal or not to gimbal'. Gimbals, that method of suspension which will enable the stove to remain horizontal no matter what angle the ship adopts, are essential to cooking afloat, and not only when cooking under way. For an exposed marina in a heavy blow can closely resemble the confused sea of a tide-way race. Gimbals will also preserve soup on calm days from the attacks of passing power boats, the wakes of inquisitive trippers or the unannounced jump of visitors on the deck above. A fully gimballed stove which can respond to pitch as well as to roll takes up a considerable space in a galley since the stove must be free of obstruction from bulkhead, hull or galley carcass in both directions. Some ocean sailing craft have solved the problem by installing two independently swung burners, gimballed in both directions, from which the separate pressurised fuel cylinders are attached to act as ballast. This solution loses both grill and oven. If there is not sufficient room for swing in both arcs, choose thwartship roll compensation first. Craft under sail list to leeward, and thwartship roll motion from wind and wave is more frequent than pitch. In some fast motor craft stoves are permanently fixed, since pitch is frequently more violent at speed. When the gimballed stove is installed, check that the centre of gravity of the largest cooking pot, when full and placed on the stove top, is below the pivot of the stove suspension. It is also necessary to fit a locking device which can immobilise the stove if required, so that cooking utensils cannot be upset by inadvertently leaning on the stove during preparation.

While considering the boat, the stove and the saucepans in motion, it is as well to envisage the cook in a similar situation. A snap ring fastening on a nearby strongpoint for the cook's safety harness, and two hand holds within easy reach from the stove, will help the cook under the most difficult conditions. Cooking so often requires two hands that the old adage of 'only one hand for the boat' does not apply in the galley. So gimbal the stove and suspend the cook.

The Source of Heat and Stove Installation

The choice of fuel for the cooker is a much debated and vexatious subject. Bottled pressurised butane or propane gas is the cleanest, most efficient, the most economical and most readily controlled source of heat on a small boat. The snag is its explosive nature when mixed with a sufficiency of air. One hears every year of boats damaged and crewmen injured by gas explosion. Probably an equal number of incidents caused by motor fuel or bad weather or just stupidity pass unnoticed in any sailing season. Such events are not so spectacular as explosion and therefore attract less publicity. But explosion can only arise from an uncontrolled escape of cooking-gas fuel. Once this potential source of danger is recognised, if the most elementary precautions are taken as an inflexible routine, then the chances of explosion are no greater than any other common result of carelessness, like striking a rock or sinking as a result of collision.

Precautions begin with a careful and correct installation. Butane and propane gas suppliers and stove manufacturers, as well as the nautical authorities and insurance companies, lay down safety standards for installation which must be followed strictly. If the pressurised gas cylinder is firmly secured in its own compartment (preferably on deck), separately vented to the air and draining over the side, remote from all electrics and as far as possible from the engine-fuel storage, then the prime source of danger is controlled. The piped supply should be as short as practicable, should consist of as few junctions and unions as possible and should be easily accessible throughout its whole length. The pipe used should be of seamless copper, in one run. Flexible metal hose and rubber tubing are less safe and require frequent inspection for renewal. The unions at the gas-cylinder valve and the stove should be sealed with the compound recommended by the manufacturers for such installations, and these should be checked regularly. This is rightly the cook's responsibility. Finally, and this must be an inflexible routine for every ship's cook and all who use the stove, *the gas must be turned off at the cylinder source after each period of use,* even though all the stove taps are off at the time. If this routine is invariably observed, then risk of explosion will be reduced to a permissible minimum. Such a rule should not pose any problem to the members of the crew. It is readily recognised that the echo sounder, electronic log, the D/F set, the radio telephone and the lights are all turned off when their use is completed. It should not be difficult to adopt the same attitude to the bottled gas cooking fuel. Of course, the situation of the cylinder storage, the chore of going out into the cockpit on a cold rainy night after a good meal or the cold trip from a warm bunk into a dew-soaked dawn to turn on the gas before the first brew of the day can be made, are discomforting obstacles to a practice which is only common sense, but without which all on board are at risk. So TURN OFF THE GAS should be the grace of every ship's cook. Three meals a day for a crew of four, with the occasional brew of coffee or tea, will consume approximately one and a half pounds weight of cooking gas per day. Pressurised bottled cooking-gas fuel is available in most sailing areas. It would be wise to ascertain the availability of supply before a protracted cruise, to carry a spare bottle, and to check the necessity for screw adaptors to adjust the ship's installed equipment to local supply cylinder threads.

Other sources of supply for heat for the cooking stove aboard are paraffin or kerosene, and methylated spirit or alcohol. Preferred by many as a safer fuel, available almost universally even in remote areas, there are many types of stove designed to burn these liquid fuels. The pressurised kerosene stove, which requires a preheating phase with alcohol or methylated spirit, is less readily controlled as a source of heat while cooking, and is susceptible during operation to draughts. It is also very smelly and dirty if not kept scrupulously clean, and it can, in its preheating phase, create vexatious situations in which squirts of unburned fuel and clouds of soot envelop the interior of the boat. Should a kerosene stove be installed, a length of fine steel wire and a tooth brush will be needed. These will enable the cook to clean the burners and to start the process of lighting the stove all over again, if patience has been preserved, to which last a hungry crew do not always contribute. Consumption of paraffin fuel for three meals a day plus hot drinks for a crew of four will average some three pints per day, together with a pint of alcohol or spirit per week – and in the hands of the inept these can make a lot of soot.

An alternative liquid fuel for the stove is methyl alcohol. One of the safest forms of heat, it is not as effective as pressurised gas. It takes longer to cook food, for as a fuel it does not produce as much heat, and consumption for a crew of four can be as much as half a gallon a day, which may present a storage problem. There are two types of alcohol stove, in one the fuel is injected through the burners under pressure, in the other the fuel is gravity fed to the stove; both require a preheating phase. The alcohol stove is the least dangerous in the hands of the forgetful and disorganised, since a fuel fire can be extinguished with water and there is no danger of explosion except under extreme circumstances. The fuel tanks of both alcohol and kerosene stoves are usually an integral part of the cooker, and filling with fuel can present a problem in boisterous conditions.

Having chosen the stove, look to its installation in the galley, to its surroundings, its light and ventilation, its protection from draughts and its accessibility for cleaning. Light and ventilation are most important to the cook and to the other occupants at meal time. The persistence of last night's curry in the breakfast air is a poor beginning to a day's sail, and the warmth of the cabin from the cooker is only welcome if untainted with the odour of cabbage. A cowled ventilator or louvred extractor above the stove is not a luxury but a necessity. The susceptibility of fibreglass hulls to condensation and the fact that cooking is a prime source of water vapour, call for serious attention to ventilation in the galley.

Light, too, is of great importance to the cook. A warm cosy glow in the cabin is poor illumination for the preparation of a meal and chopped onion is easily contaminated with flesh and blood in a dim light. A single light behind the cook's head as he stands at the galley produces gloom in the cooking area from his shadow. Two sources of light above the galley, one on the left and the other to the right of the cook, will illuminate a shadow-free area for preparation and cooking, so that what goes into the pot will be clearly seen. The accessibility of the stove for cleaning is so often forgotten that it may be assumed that galley layout designers have never seen milk boil over or soup spill. There should be at least a four-inch space around the back and both sides of any stove. If the galley carcass is covered in, the stove area with a heat-proof asbestos lining, this should be covered with a detachable aluminium facing. Asbestos sheet absorbs spilled liquids and splashed fat, and is difficult to clean. A metal covering is easily wiped down after each cooking period. The stale smell of many a galley comes from the fireproofing liner, which cannot be cleaned.

Safety Measures and Fire Extinguishers

No matter what type of stove is fitted, a fire extinguisher must be within easy reach from the galley. It must not be fitted above the stove, for it should not be necessary to put the hand through the source of the fire to reach the extinguisher. There are three common types, the CO_2, the dry powder and the chemical gas extinguisher. The CO_2 extinguisher is very effective and can be recharged easily after use. It is, however, a bulky piece of equipment, is heavy to use and is very messy. The powder-type extinguisher is lighter, is very efficient and is simple to use; it is very messy, as well. Activated by a CO_2 cartridge it is possible to examine the contents regularly and to recharge the extinguisher. The extinguisher should be shaken fairly often to agitate the powder which tends to pack by sedimentation if left undisturbed for a long period. It is well to bear in mind that the extinguisher powder is lethal to the moving parts of machinery. If a powder extinguisher has been used, the engine compartment, engine and particularly air intakes should be vacuum cleaned before the engine is run. The gas-filled extinguishers are of three types. The carbon tetrachloride type is not suitable on a boat. The fumes are poisonous and in a confined space, such as a cabin, can be lethal. The others use BCF or Dupont FE 1301. These extinguishers are extremely efficient, act rapidly and extinguish any fire (except the white signal flare!). They have the advantage that, installed in various strategic positions, they can be remotely activated. Light and easy to use, clean in operation and non-toxic they are probably the best choice for cabin use. Crew should not remain for more than a few minutes in a confined space if the extinguisher has been used, as concentrations over 5 per cent can cause dizziness.

It is much less important to argue the respective merits of the various types than to ensure that the crew are versed in their use, and know the position of the extinguishers, even in the dark. With the co-operation of the local fire brigade, a practice with the fire extinguisher ashore could be a vital part of fitting out. Do not leave it until too late to familiarise those on board with the method of using the extinguishers. The fire may not be bright enough to read the instructions on the extinguisher when the emergency occurs.

The Sink

The second item common to most galleys is the sink, though it is not essential; two plastic bowls used in the cockpit are just as effective and are considered by many sailing men to be superior since they do not require skin fittings. If sink there be then it must be a sink in size and not an enlarged soap dish. It should be of stainless steel and a water supply should be an integral part of the fitment. Size is of paramount importance. The sink must be large enough to take the tableware items commonly used at meals. The average dinner plate is 10½ in. in diameter. A sink only 8 in. across is an abomination. Above all the sink must be deep; deep enough to hold a gallon of water at least. Even when half full it should be possible to immerse cups and mugs so that the washing of crockery can be achieved even in a popple. It is possible to purchase the stainless steel type of basin used on inter-city railroad sleeping cars, which has an incurved rim. Under unstable conditions this retains the washing water. The capacity of the sink does not affect fresh water consumption since it is usual for sea water to be used for this purpose, a fresh water rinse being sufficient. There is no satisfactory alternative material to stainless steel for the yacht's sink. The surface of all plastic materials, popular in caravans, will scratch, and beetroot, curry and pickled walnut will stain the surface. Those scourers which keep stainless steel bright and clean will ruin a plastic surface in no time.

Fresh water may be supplied to the basin by gravity feed or by hand or electric pump. Whatever the method it must be possible to put not only cups and glasses but also jugs and kettles under the spout of the tap or faucet. A short spout set back from the sink edge will deliver water to the sink or to a tooth mug but will not fill a jug or a pressure cooker. The ideal type is the rotatable tubular tap which can be swivelled to move over and beyond the basin and which will deliver water to the largest receptacle. Drainage will rapidly show any inefficiency by smell and failure to empty the sink. The shortest straightest line from sink vent to boat's skin is the only route. All bends, curves and kinks are potential traps causing blockage and its odoriferous accompaniment. Like all skin fittings the drain outlet must have a stop cock. When going to windward the involuntary supply of sea water on the sink-side tack does not improve sailing performance.

Fresh Water Supply on Board

The supply of fresh water to the galley is of first importance both to the comfort of the crew and to good cooking aboard. The greatest drain upon this supply is the sink. This is true both literally and figuratively. The greatest waste comes from such simple operations as pumping water to rinse a glass or wash a lettuce under the tap. It is all so very quick and easy.

Yet surrounded by water, even in port, one can still be short of fresh drinking water, particularly if cruising in strange areas. On some small cruisers the day's supply is drawn off into plastic containers so that consumption may be easily and visually measured. Other boats economise by using sea water for washing up and for cooking potatoes or shell fish. Sea water for this purpose should be drawn at least five miles from shore, and even five miles may mean little more than dilution of sewage in some areas. A fairly reliable guide to the cleanliness of the sea water can be obtained firstly from its clarity and secondly from the healthy growth of marine life on the tide's edge. Death and decay in animal and vegetable is the litmus guide to pollution of the sea.

If cruising in foreign parts it is wise at first to treat any fresh-water source with suspicion. Supplies from marina water-points are usually reliable, but any supply anywhere which does not come from a pressurised main should be viewed with caution, and water from open wells must be classified as instant dysentery. If at all uncertain as to purity, treat the water with sterilising tablets. If there are young children aboard it is wise before use to boil water used for drinking, as tender stomachs are easily upset.

On some boats the sink is reserved for the crew's personal toilet, plastic bowls being substituted for food preparation and dish washing. For much of the sailing season culinary activities can be performed in the cockpit as communal chores. The worst of the galley tasks, the washing up, is completed quickly and easily by the crew if a production line is formed in the cockpit. A bowl of hot sea water with a bowl of fresh water to rinse and a space to drain the crocks will spread the work. If at the conclusion of the washing process, the bowl of dirty sea water is emptied into the bowl of rinsing water, the fugitive tea spoon, which would otherwise have been poured over the side, will be discovered before it is too late. Such a piece of organised team work saves time and tea spoons.

The Stove/Sink Unit as a Working Area

The sink and stove are generally incorporated into a galley frame or carcass. Too often the sink is situated immediately next to the stove, making it easy to splash from the sink into the frying pan contents or to burn oneself on a kettle when washing up in the sink. It is a great advantage if the stove and sink are separated by a worktop space, which will be increased during preparation of the meal by the cover lid of the stove and during serving by the lid of the sink. No disposition should be accepted where the cook needs to reach across the stove to use the sink. There are similar disadvantages and a waste of space where the cooker abuts on to the sink at right angles. The cooking stove and sink should either be in line or in parallel, with standing space between. Fire and water should be well apart, for the chances of burns on the hands or the more dangerous flare-up caused by water splashing into hot fat or frying oil are too great to risk. The finest arrangements incorporate cooker, refrigerator or ice-box and sink in line in that order. This provides the maximum working space and separation within one unit.

The placement of the galley unit within the hull is as difficult as any complicated jig-saw puzzle. Opposite the dinette on the starboard side is favoured by many, since it puts the cooking area close to the eating area around the table. A central table situation with seats either side shifts the galley away from the centre of the cabin, and a thwartship disposition results. Where the companionway is offset to one side of the cabin trunk, the stove/sink area immediately upon one's hand on entry is favoured by those who insist on maximum ventilation above the galley which the main hatch supplies. This location is also subject to draughts. Users of paraffin or spirit stoves note and beware.

Ventilation and light are as important above the sink as over the stove. The previously recommended two lights for the galley will solve the visibility problem at night. An opening port over the sink will admit daylight and will also allow steam from cooking and draining pots to escape, otherwise condensation rapidly forms on the hull interior.

Tailpiece

The Polyestermite

Bill Beavis

The author writes as follows:

'*The polyestermite was first released on the boating public
in 1970 when* Yachting and Boating (*a magazine since
defunct*) *published this article in its London Boat Show
issue. The hoax took off and we had scores of readers
coming up to the magazine's stand to ask if such a
creature existed. Within weeks the story had spread.
Boatbuilders were being quizzed by worried owners, other
readers belonging to other magazines were phoning their
editors, even the Natural History Museum rang up. By
summer the enquiries had gone international and poly-
estermites were responsible for new harbour buoys disap-
pearing in Durban, for ruining one country's Admiral's
Cup chances, and even disrupting the oil flow at some
Gulf port.*

'*One person, at least, enjoyed the joke: a wooden boat-
builder from British Columbia wrote asking for a jar of
polyestermite tadpoles.*'

'I think you may be interested in my discovery.' That was as much as the Lloyds surveyor would tell me on the telephone. Hardly the sort of invitation to lure one down to the coast on a wintry afternoon – except that I detected a special note of urgency in his voice.

We had arranged to meet near the boat hoist, but when I arrived at the yard he was already by the gate, jam jar in hand.

'Look at this,' he grated, thrusting his arm through the car window. The jar he was holding contained a small prawn-like creature.

'What is it?' I asked, being largely mistrustful of seafood.

'It's a *polyestermite*,' he boasted proudly. 'The first one we've managed to catch in this country.'

'Well, well . . . that's really exciting.' I offered cautiously. 'If there's one subject certain to bring me racing to the coast without my lunch, it's insectology. I'm mad about bugs. So what does it do, eat turnips or something?'

'No, glassfibre, as a matter of fact. *It eats glassfibre boats.*'

He led me across to an infested boat which was lying in her cradle. 'This is where we found the little horror,' he explained, and banged the hull with his hammer. A shower of white powder fell to the ground.

'You mean to say they've done this!' The hull looked to me like a section drawing through an ant colony.

'Yes,' he replied. 'In three days. She was as sound as a bell when the owner left her on Sunday. When he comes down on Friday he'll be able to sweep her away with a broom.'

I dusted my shoulders already covered with left-overs and droppings, sat down and listened while he told me the whole incredible story.

It appears that, with the demise of wooden boats, the common gribble or shipworm began to go hungry. There was a great migration to wooden piers, wharves and things like that, but soon these were all eaten up and starvation followed. Eventually and inevitably there was cannibalism, a situation in which only the toughest of the species would survive. Not only did the toughest survive, but the sinister creatures actually grew stronger and larger due to the hormone-rich diet their mates had provided; soon we had a super-gribble on our hands.

Opinions are divided as to the precise stage when the super-gribble evolved into the *polyestermite* but, in a relatively short period of time, Nature adapted itself to man's preference for glassfibre (cleans with a damp cloth!) and gave this new species the facility with which to eat it. In chemical terms this was a masticatory-assisted gland containing a powerful solvent acid. The acid, which chemists have found to be a hundred times stronger than nail varnish remover, is excreted onto the gel coat and then dispersed by the insect's feet – it will be noticed that some of the fore legs are shaped like glue spreaders for the purpose. The acid soon dissolves the gel coat and the creature is quickly through to the chopped strand mat, or the woven rovings, which of course it enjoys best. It is a prolific eater and can, during a feeding frenzy such as the mating season when it needs a lot of energy, eat four times its own weight.

The *polyestermite* (or *resinus pestus domestos*) was first discovered in America where it was found eating plastic detergent bottles on the Hudson River, a splendid début which instantly endeared it to the Friends of the Earth Society. Very quickly they were marketing T-shirts with the little crustacean on the front. Indeed it was a rapturous beginning, and a Wisconsin candidate, running for Congress on a conservation ticket, even adopted the *polyestermite* as his motif. But then somebody found them quietly chewing away on the recently laid Alaskan pipeline, and the honey-moon promptly ended.

Despite strict surveillance at the ports and a ban imposed by the Ministry of Agriculture and Fisheries, the *polyestermite* came to Britain some time last winter. Already it is firmly established along the south coast, where its notoriety has even overshadowed the fast growing Japanese seaweed. So far no effective antidote has been found, although everything including banned insecticides has been tried – it actually *enjoys* some of the better known proprietary brands.

And now there is one more alarming fact which has just been discovered. Government scientists working at the Germ Warfare Establishment at Porton Down near Salisbury have found that the *polyestermite* is biologically *double-ended*. That is to say it has a mouth at each end so, with mandibles at the front and nippers at the rear, it can lie on its back in a marina and eat two boats at once.

I asked the Lloyds surveyor if there was anything, just anything, which owners could do to protect their boats from the ravages of this pest. There was only one sure remedy, he said, expensive but totally effective.

'And what is that?' I demanded anxiously.

'Sheathe the boat in wood.'

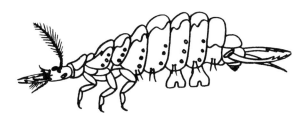

Fig. 42 The Polyestermite (Resinus Pestus Domestos)

Lee Shore
This sequence of pictures dramatically illustrates the meaning of the words 'lee shore'. These were taken by Edward Tadros: the boat shown was reduced to matchwood less than an hour after grounding on the coast of Normandy. The pictures were included in Richard Henderson's book on seamanship, Sea Sense, *published by Adlard Coles Limited in 1975.*

Well Spun Yarns:
Classic Sailing Narratives

The Young Viking

James Henderson
Sloops and Brigs
first published 1972

Adlard Coles Ltd published two books by James Henderson on the Royal Navy during the Napoleonic Wars, Frigates *and* Sloops and Brigs. *He died in 1971, when a third book, which was to have been called* Ships of the Line, *was in preparation. The period he describes was surely the Royal Navy's greatest era, when victories against numerically superior forces were regularly achieved, and the Navy stood unchallenged in its supremacy across the oceans of the world. James Henderson describes outstanding actions fought at this time with a zest for the period and an eye for technical accuracy which bring the incidents alive. This extract from* Sloops and Brigs, *which covers the smallest ships in the RN, describes the cruise of the* SPEEDY, *culminating in what the author terms 'perhaps the most astounding single-ship encounter in all recorded history'. One convention should be noted: the names of RN ships are printed in* SMALL CAPITALS, *and those of enemy forces in italics.*

Thomas, Lord Cochrane, was one of 'fortune's favourites'. Not only was he son and heir of the ninth Earl of Dundonald, his uncle, Sir Archibald Cochrane, was a distinguished naval officer. His father had served in the Navy, but would rather his son had joined the Army; however, the young man's mind was quite determined on the Navy, and eventually he joined as a midshipman under his uncle, setting foot for the first time on the deck of a warship in June 1793, at the advanced age (for a midshipman) of seventeen years. However, the care of his uncle had put him 'on the books' five years earlier, thus defeating the careful regulations of Samuel Pepys, and enabling him to be appointed acting lieutenant before he was twenty, years before he ever saw a shot fired in anger. Thirsting for service and command, he could never forget that at twenty Nelson was a post captain.

Cochrane was in many ways typical of the Lowland Scottish aristocracy, of Norse origin. Very tall, and even as a young man of a commanding presence, he was well aware of 'the deference due to a man of pedigree'. Where that deference was paid, he was the most affable and charming man imaginable; but he was fiercely resentful of anything resembling a stretch of authority by his seniors in the service. Before action he would gravely consider all the factors; when action was decided on, he was as fierce and headlong as any of his Berserker ancestors, yet always cool and watchful for any circumstance of which he might make use. A 'mariner of infinite resource and sagacity', an ideal commander, but a prickly subordinate.

After service in various ships he found himself, at the end of 1798, a lieutenant on board the BARFLEUR, the flag-ship of Lord Keith (also a Scotsman), Commander-in-Chief of the Mediterranean Fleet. This was the usual position from which 'fortune's favourites' could expect fairly early promotion to commander. Discipline on a flag-ship was always strict, with much formality on the quarter-deck, and First Lieutenant Philip Beaver was the very man to enforce it. He took occasion to reprimand Cochrane in the wardroom, and Cochrane gave offence, not so much by his words but by his disdainful demeanour. Beaver immediately demanded a court-martial on Cochrane, which could not be refused. The details are too tedious to recount, and indeed the Admiral found the same. Cochrane was acquitted of whatever he was accused of and advised to respect the position of a first lieutenant, but Beaver was rebuked for his methods; the whole fleet had been delayed a day, when the wind had come fair and they might have been a hundred miles on their way, and this for the most trivial complaint. Beaver, however, was soon promoted post captain, and served with some distinction, dying at the Cape of Good Hope in 1814. Early in 1800 Keith made Cochrane commander in the gun-brig-sloop SPEEDY, and no doubt felt easier for having cleared his quarter-deck of both a martinet and a firebrand.

The SPEEDY was quite small for her class, being 158 tons, with a crew of 6 officers and 84 men; only 2 of the officers were commissioned, Cochrane and his lieutenant, Richard William Parker, the officers otherwise being of warrant rank. The quarters must have been uncommonly tight, for the tonnage only comes to 1¾ tons per man, the least I am aware of; a frigate had about 4 tons per man. She could only carry 10 tons of water, about 25 gallons per man, so that she had to re-water every few weeks. The commander's cabin was not big enough for a chair, being entirely occupied by a table surrounded by lockers, forming both storage and seating. The headroom was only five feet, making it difficult for a man of Cochrane's height to get in at all; and when it came to shaving, he had to lift off the skylight, stand up through the opening and set out his tackle on the quarter-deck. Her armament was minute – fourteen long 4-pounders, throwing a shot about the size of a cricket ball. On one occasion Cochrane walked the quarter-deck with a whole broadside – seven shot – of his ship in his coat pockets. Cochrane asked for, and was allowed, two 12-pounder long guns as fore and stern chasers; but there was not room enough to work them, and the timbers would not stand the recoil. Later he asked for 6-pounders instead of his 4s, but the ports were not big enough. The only 'improvement' he was able to make was in his rig: the mainyard requiring to be replaced, a spar was supplied longer than the original; it was ordered to be cut down to size, but instead of doing so Cochrane had the end planed so as to make it appear that it had been cut, and got away with it, so that he could spread in his main course and main-topsail more canvas than the ship was designed for. This may or may not be an improvement. It would appear that Cochrane was under the vulgar delusion that the more sail you hoist the faster you can go. In fact length on the waterline is the limiting factor, and once the optimum sail area for length has been reached, more canvas will by no means increase the speed, but rather decrease it by depressing the bow. The design of sailing ships, indeed of any ship, is a very complicated business, and it is best to accept the ship as it comes from the yard; but then Cochrane always felt that he could do a little better, and history shows that in matters he fully understood this was true.

Cochrane was very proud of his first command. He had not much to survey, but he was monarch as far as it went. This precisely suited him, and he soon endeared himself to his men by his steady but kindly discipline, his care for their comfort, or rather to alleviate their discomforts, and the occasional treat such as fresh vegetables when in port, not only pleasing the men but keeping them healthy and alert. He exercised them at the guns far beyond the Admiralty allowance of powder and shot for practice, and trained them in boarding tactics. Very soon he had a keen and compact company, trained to his hand, eager to do anything he set them at.

The first order was a small convoy job, which was neatly executed, beating off some gun-boats and capturing a French privateer in 1800, bringing the convoy of 14 ships safely into Leghorn. He then rejoined Lord Keith off Genoa, where the French under Massena were occupying the town. Soon, by capitulation, Massena gave up the town and retreated to Nice, and Keith gave Cochrane the orders which exactly suited him – to cruise on the coast of Spain and attack anything in sight. SPEEDY had a wonderful time all June and July, sending seven or eight prizes into Leghorn, where the SPEEDY anchored on August 3rd. Lord Keith was highly pleased with the enthusiasm and success of his compatriot, and invited him to share all the festivities which happened to be going on ashore. In a fortnight SPEEDY was at sea again, with orders to harass the coast of Spain but not to risk his vessel against heavy stuff. However, after capturing a small privateer, they fell in with the MUTINE, under a post captain who had a number of French prisoners on board; he ordered Cochrane to take these on board and ship them to Leghorn, which he did rather sulkily, and remained at Leghorn until 14th September, refitting. On the 22nd he captured a large Neapolitan vessel with a French prize crew on board, and brought her into Port Mahon on 5th October. Here he was informed that the depredations of the SPEEDY had attracted the attention of the Spanish authorities, who were fitting out a frigate especially to 'abate the nuisance'. Now the 'infinite resource and sagacity' began to show. There was in the Mediterranean a Danish brig, the *Clomer*, not unlike the SPEEDY: Cochrane painted the SPEEDY in the *Clomer*'s colours, found a Dane somehow and appointed him quartermaster, and found him a Danish naval officer's uniform. The SPEEDY sailed from Port Mahon into the worst winter weather in living memory, and found very little reward. On 21st December a vessel was sighted, which appeared a large and deep-laden merchantman; but as they neared she hoisted Spanish colours and opened her ports to show a formidable battery. SPEEDY hoisted Danish colours, but the Spaniard signalled her to heave-to, and lowered a boat. SPEEDY complied, and also ran up the quarantine flag. When the boat came alongside, the Danish quartermaster explained that this was the *Clomer*, two days out from Algiers, where the plague was known to be raging; but the officer could come on board and see for himself. The invitation was declined, and the ships parted company. The Spaniard was the *Gamo*, a xebec-rigged frigate. Xebec denotes any ship with square sails forward and lateen aft; usually they are quite small coasters, but the *Gamo* was a small frigate of over 600 tons, with two masts square-rigged and a lateen on the mizzen. Her force has been sometimes exaggerated, but in fact she was very much the equivalent of a British sixth-rate 28-gun frigate, mounting twenty-two long 12-pounders on the main deck and eight long 8-pounders and 2 carronades, 24-pounders, on quarter-deck and forecastle, but with a much larger crew than the British equivalent, 319 against 194. Obviously, with a six-to-one superiority, she could eat up the SPEEDY at one mouthful; yet some of the officers of the brig thought they would have liked to have a go at her. Cochrane promised he would think about it, and if it were at all feasible there might be another meeting.

SPEEDY kept on cruising between Cartagena and Barcelona, with great success, coming into Port Mahon on the 24th January with a convoy of prizes. Thence she made for Malta, where Cochrane got himself involved in a silly duel with a French officer of the Royalists, who were there on the Allied side. Fortunately neither was killed, for there were present all the elements of an 'Allied' split. No doubt a Royalist French officer had laid hands upon Cochrane at a fancy dress ball, when he was disguised as a British tar; and to lay hands on a Scottish gentleman is death, naturally: but there were provocations. On the whole, the incident tended to strengthen the establishment view that Cochrane, although a bonny fighter, was a danger to authority, known to be of a Whig family and probably a Radical. This was in fact true, and he remained so all his life; but of course events overtook him and the Radical of 1800 became the staunch establishment of 1860.

Another profitable cruise on the coast of Spain left the SPEEDY with a crew of only 54, due to the prize crews sent with the captured ships to Port Mahon. Off Barcelona a large ship was sighted sailing close under the land, and she was eventually made out to be the *Gamo*. Cochrane piped all hands, told them what was before them, and gave his orders. As the ships approached the *Gamo* fired a gun and hoisted her Spanish colours, the usual way of demanding that a strange ship should identify herself. The SPEEDY hoisted American colours and continued to approach. In the odd sort of sea-etiquette of the period it was perfectly all right to show false colours so long as one hoisted the true colours before opening fire; to fire under false colours laid the whole crew open to the penalties of piracy. The Spaniard hesitated long enough for the SPEEDY to go about on the other tack, when she ran up the British ensign, and the *Gamo* fired a broadside without hitting anything. A second time she fired, also without effect; while the SPEEDY came on in perfect silence, until she ran alongside and locked her yards in the Spaniard's rigging.

This manoeuvre was not bravado: during the previous encounter Cochrane had taken a long look at the *Gamo*, and had noted that not only was her main battery mounted fairly high, her ports did not allow for the guns being depressed. The low-velocity cannon of the period needed a high trajectory to carry any distance; it was a matter of tossing the shot rather than shooting it with velocity. If the port were made large enough to allow of depressing the gun as well as elevating it there would be very little bulwark left to give an impression of protection to the gun-crew. Locked alongside, the SPEEDY was so small and so low in the water that the shot of the *Gamo* roared through her rigging, with damage to the cordage and sails but very little to her men; whereas the little guns of the SPEEDY, being elevated and double-shotted, sent their light shot smashing up through the sides and deck with such effect that the first broadside killed the captain and boatswain. The Spanish next-in-command saw his disadvantage, and gave the order for boarding, which was heard just as clearly on the SPEEDY. When the Spaniards were assembled for boarding, the SPEEDY sheered off, and put a broadside and a volley of musketry into the close ranks. Again and a third time was this manoeuvre repeated, until the Spaniards gave up the idea of boarding and stood to their guns, however little effective.

This, however, could not continue; the SPEEDY was in exactly the position of the lady who went for a ride on a tiger; as long as she remained close enough she could get along well enough, but she could not get away. Cochrane determined to board the *Gamo* with all hands. The surgeon, Mr Guthrie (descended, I believe, from a locally famous Covenanter family), volunteered to take the tiller, and with two or possibly three boys formed the whole ship's complement. With admirable skill he laid the SPEEDY right alongside the *Gamo*, and the boarders leapt up her side, one party at the head and the other at the waist, which was as far as the SPEEDY extended. The boarders at the head had been ordered to blacken their faces and generally make themselves look like pirates, and when they emerged through the gun smoke, yelling like fiends, the Spaniards wavered for a moment; and in that moment they were assailed in flank and rear by the main party. Seeing an opportunity, Cochrane sent a hand to haul down the Spanish colours; the Spaniards supposed that their officers had surrendered the ship, and laid down their arms. It was a legend in the Navy that the surrender was expedited by Cochrane calling to the SPEEDY 'Send another fifty men!' to which the surgeon replied 'Fifty men – aye aye Sir!'

All troubles were not over, for the unwounded prisoners numbered about 270, almost seven times the unwounded of the SPEEDY. The officers were transferred to the sloop, and the men battened down under hatches; but there must have been very little sleep for Cochrane and his men during the next few days, until they brought their big prize into Port Mahon.

This was perhaps the most astounding single-ship encounter in all recorded history. There have been cases where the weaker ship has defended herself courageously, and sometimes successfully; but never before or since has a ship actually attacked another of an altogether superior class, and conquered. The bare statistics show the amazing disparity of force:

	SPEEDY	*Gamo*
Tonnage	158	Over 600
Main-deck guns	14, 4-pounders	22, 12-pounders
Quarter-deck guns	None	8, 8-pounders, 2 carronades, 24s
Weight of broadside	28 pounds	190 pounds
Total crew	54	319

Of these crews, the SPEEDY lost three killed and nine wounded, including Lieutenant Parker; the *Gamo* 14 killed, including her captain, and 41 wounded, total 55 casualties, one more than the whole crew with which the SPEEDY went into action.

The news of this astonishing action was rapturously received in England, but Authority was quite cool about it. There was no haste to promote Cochrane post captain, which had rewarded many lesser victors. It may be that Authority felt that the risk was too great and should not have been taken, disregarding the months of thought that had gone into the problem. There may have been jealousy of Cochrane's success, both in glory and in prize-money: in the year's cruise the humblest seaman in the SPEEDY had earned more in prize-money than the regular pay of almost any officer. At any rate, Cochrane's next job was to go peaceably to Algiers to expostulate with the Dey about the seizure of a merchant ship, surely a task more suitable for a civilian diplomat, and unsuccessful.

Once more Cochrane was sent to cruise off the coast of Spain, and almost at once captured a Spanish privateer of 8 guns. This he fitted out as a tender to the SPEEDY, and gave the command to his young brother Midshipman the Hon. Archibald Cochrane, who had been with him throughout his service in the ship; a decidedly high-handed proceeding which was unlikely to endear him to Authority. Later they fell in with the KANGAROO, Captain Pulling, and under his orders engaged in a fierce and protracted battle with ships and forts at Oropesa, until they had expended almost all their shot after nine hours' firing, for the SPEEDY could only load 1,400 shot. They now ran in as if to board the ships and attack the fort by land, at which the defenders of the fort 'retired in confusion' and the ships ran themselves ashore; three of them, however, were brought off.

When Cochrane returned with his usual clutch of prizes to Port Mahon he found, to his intense chagrin, that the *Gamo* had not been bought into the service but had been sold very cheaply to the Dey of Algiers. He had confidently hoped that it would have been bought in and that after repair he would command it as a post captain, and again he suspected official jealousy. This may have been an element, but more probably the xebec did not fit at all into the rigging system. Apart from the lateen-rigged mizzen, the sail arrangements on the two square-rigged masts were quite different from anything in British sail lofts. Cochrane's view was that this was all to the good; the lateen rig had proved itself for a thousand years to be the handiest for coasting in the Mediterranean, and the totally un-British appearance was a far better camouflage than a Danish quartermaster.

The next assignment was less rewarding: to convoy a very slow-sailing packet ship with mails to Gibraltar. However, he relieved the tedium by examining all the anchorages along the coast, and came upon a few merchant ships near Alicante. They ran themselves ashore: it would take too long to bring them off, so Cochrane fired them. One of them was laden with oil, and produced a tremendous blaze which, on a very dark night, was visible over a wide area. This attracted the attention of a squadron of three French ships of the line making for the Atlantic, and at five o'clock on the morning of 3rd July 1801 they fell in with the SPEEDY. For four hours they coursed her like greyhounds with a hare, while Cochrane tried every dodge his inventive brain could devise. He had all his guns thrown overboard, and indeed it would have been unwise to have fired them, since the view of the day on the laws of warfare was that it was quite wrong, even criminal, to shoot when there was no possible hope of success. Away went the anchors and the boats, while the SPEEDY tacked and wore and dodged without success; the big French ships were faster and almost as handy, and at length she came under the broadside of the *Desaix*, and the cruise of the SPEEDY was over.

Cochrane never commanded a brig again, because after he was exchanged he eventually got his post rank. His subsequent career as a frigate captain I have related in *The Frigates*, and his later services are part of South American history; but we may have a glimpse of him at the end of his career, when he was the tenth Earl of Dundonald, Admiral and Commander-in-Chief, North American station. From the local newspaper in Bermuda, 21st May 1850:

> On Thursday last the noble Earl, the Commander-in-Chief of the Navy, gave a ball, in His Lordship's usual magnificent style, to above 350 persons – comprising the élite of these Islands . . . The ball was a full dress one; and His Lordship, in full uniform – covered with orders, won in many a desperate encounter – stood to welcome a crowd of guests. Many beheld for the first time this distinguished hero – His Lordship appeared in excellent health and spirits, delighting all with his good humour and urbanity.

A Tintack Victory

Joshua Slocum
Sailing Alone Around the World
first published 1900 (Mariners Library 1955)

The remaining extracts, apart from the 'tailpiece', are from titles published in the Mariners Library series by Rupert Hart-Davis, an imprint closely linked with Adlard Coles Ltd since the early 1960's. The idea of the list was to reprint celebrated sailing narratives, many of which were long out of print and otherwise unobtainable. Sailing Alone Around the World *was an inevitable choice, and the book is far too well-known for us not to include a short, amusing incident from it.*

The *Spray's* good luck followed fast. I discovered, as she sailed along through a labyrinth of islands, that she was in the Cockburn Channel, which leads into the Strait of Magellan at a point opposite Cape Froward, and that she was already passing Thieves' Bay, suggestively named. And at night, March 8, behold, she was at anchor in a snug cove at the Turn! Every heartbeat on the *Spray* now counted thanks.

Here I pondered on the events of the last few days, and, strangely enough, instead of feeling rested from sitting or lying down, I now began to feel jaded and worn; but a hot meal of venison stew soon put me right, so that I could sleep. As drowsiness came on I sprinkled the deck with tacks, and then I turned in, bearing in mind the advice of my old friend Samblich that I was not to step on them myself. I saw to it that not a few of them stood 'business end' up; for when the *Spray* passed Thieves' Bay two canoes had put out and followed in her wake, and there was no disguising the fact any longer that I was alone.

Fig. 43 'They howled like a pack of hounds'

Now, it is well known that one cannot step on a tack without saying something about it. A pretty good Christian will whistle when he steps on the 'commercial end' of a carpet-tack; a savage will howl and claw the air, and that was just what happened that night about twelve o'clock, while I was asleep in the cabin, where the savages thought they 'had me,' sloop and all, but changed their minds when they stepped on deck, for then they thought that I or somebody else had them. I had no need of a dog; they howled like a pack of hounds. I had hardly use for a gun. They jumped pell-mell, some into their canoes and some into the sea, to cool off, I suppose, and there was a deal of free language over it as they went. I fired several guns when I came on deck, to let the rascals know that I was home, and then I turned in again, feeling sure I should not be disturbed any more by people who left in so great a hurry.

The Fuegians, being cruel, are naturally cowards; they regard a rifle with superstitious fear. The only real danger one could see that might come from their quarter would be from allowing them to surround one within bow-shot, or to anchor within range where they might lie in ambush. As for their coming on deck at night, even had I not put tacks about, I could have cleared them off by shots from the cabin and hold. I always kept a quantity of ammunition within reach in the hold and in the cabin and in the forepeak, so that retreating to any of these places I could 'hold the fort' simply by shooting up through the deck.

Davies

Erskine Childers
The Riddle of the Sands
first published 1903 (Mariners Library 1955)

Erskine Childers' classic sailing thriller needs little introduction. It is one of the few fiction sailing books to sell well year after year. Interest in it enjoyed a new lease of life recently when the story was adapted to make a feature film. This extract introduces us to the incorrigible Davies, and charts the descent of Carruthers from flannels and blazer to the rather more primitive style of 'corinthian yachting'.

As I dressed into flannels and blazer, I looked round the deck, and with an unskilled and doubtful eye took in all that the darkness had hitherto hidden. She seemed very small (in point of fact she was seven tons), something over thirty feet in length and nine in beam, a size very suitable to weekends in the Solent for such as liked that sort of thing; but that she should have come from Dover to the Baltic suggested a world of physical endeavour of which I had never dreamed. I passed to the aesthetic side. Smartness and beauty were essential to yachts, in my mind, but with the best resolves to be pleased I found little encouragement here. The hull seemed too low, and the main-mast too high; the cabin roof looked clumsy, and the skylights saddened the eye with dull iron and plebeian graining. What brass there was, on the tiller-head and elsewhere, was tarnished with sickly green. The decks had none of that creamy purity which Cowes expects, but were rough and grey, and showed tarry exhalations round the seams and rusty stains near the bows. The ropes and rigging were in mourning when contrasted with the delicate buff manilla so satisfying to the artistic eye as seen against the blue of a June sky at Southsea. Nor was the whole effect bettered by many signs of recent refitting. An impression of paint, varnish and carpentry were in the air; a gaudy new burgee fluttered aloft; there seemed to be a new rope or two, especially round the diminutive mizzen-mast which itself looked altogether new. But all this only emphasised the general plainness, reminding one of a respectable woman of the working-classes trying to dress above her station, and soon likely to give it up.

That the *ensemble* was businesslike and solid even my untrained eye could see. Many of the deck fittings seemed disproportionately substantial. The anchor-chain looked contemptuous of its charge; the binnacle with its compass was of a size and prominence almost comically impressive, and was moreover the only piece of brass which was burnished and showed traces of reverent care. Two huge coils of stout and dingy warp lay just abaft the main mast, and summed up the weather-beaten aspect of the little ship. I should add here that in the distant past she had been a lifeboat, and had been clumsily converted into a yacht by the addition of a counter, deck, and the necessary spars. She was built, as all lifeboats are, diagonally, of two skins of teak, and thus had immense strength, though, in the matter of looks, all a hybrid's failings.

★   ★   ★

My night's rest and the 'ascent from the bath' had in fact done little to prepare me for contact with sharp edges and hard surfaces. But Davies had suddenly come to himself, and with an 'I say, are you comfortable? Have something to sit on?' jerked the helm a little to windward, felt it like a pulse for a moment with a rapid look to windward, and dived below, whence he returned with a couple of cushions which he threw to me. I felt perversely resentful of these luxuries and asked:

'Can't I be of any use?'

'Oh, don't you bother,' he answered. 'I expect you're tired. Aren't we having a splendid sail? That must be Ekken on the port bow,' peering under the sail, 'where the trees run in. I say, do you mind looking at the chart?' He tossed it over to me. I spread it out painfully, for it curled up like a watch-spring at the least slackening of pressure. I was not familiar with charts, and this sudden trust reposed in me after a good deal of neglect made me nervous.

'You see Flensburg, don't you?' he said. 'That's where we are,' dabbing with a long reach at an indefinite space on the crowded sheet. 'Now, which side of that buoy off the point do we pass?'

I had scarcely taken in which was land and which was water, much less the significance of the buoy, when he resumed:

'Never mind, I'm pretty sure it's all deep water about here. I expect that mark's the fairway for steamers.'

In a minute or two we were passing the buoy in question, on the wrong side I am pretty certain, for weeds and sand came suddenly into view below us with uncomfortable distinctness. But all Davies said was:

'There's never any sea here, and the plate's not down,' a dark utterance which I pondered doubtfully. 'The best of these Schleswig waters,' he went on, 'is that a boat of this size can go almost anywhere. There's no navigation required. Why—' At this moment a faint scraping was felt rather than heard beneath us.

'Aren't we aground?' I asked with great calmness.

'Oh, she'll blow over,' he replied, wincing a little.

She 'blew over,' but the episode caused a little naïve vexation in Davies. I relate it as a good instance of one of his minor peculiarities. He was utterly without that didactic pedantry which yachting has a fatal tendency to engender in men who profess it. He had tossed me the chart without a thought that I was an ignoramus, to whom it would be Greek, and who would provide him with an admirable subject to drill and lecture, just as his neglect of me throughout the morning had been merely habitual and unconscious independence. In the second place, master of his *métier*, as I knew him afterwards to be, resourceful, skilful, and alert, he was liable to lapse into a certain amateurish vagueness, half irritating and half amusing. I think truly that both these peculiarities came from the same source – a hatred of any sort of affection. To the same source I traced the fact that he and his yacht observed none of the superficial etiquette of yachts and yachtsmen, that she never, for instance, flew a national ensign, and he never wore a 'yachting suit.'

We rounded a low green point which I had scarcely noticed before.

'We must jibe,' said Davies; 'just take the helm, will you'; and, without waiting for my co-operation, he began hauling in the mainsheet with great vigour. I had rude notions of steering, but jibing is a delicate operation. No yachtsman will be surprised to hear that the boom saw its opportunity and swung over with a mighty crash, with the mainsheet entangled round me and the tiller.

'Jibed all standing,' was his sorrowful comment. 'You're not used to her yet. She's very quick on the helm.'

'Where am I to steer for?' I asked wildly.

'Oh, don't trouble, I'll take her now,' he replied.

I felt it was time to make my position clear. 'I'm an utter duffer at sailing,' I began. 'You'll have a lot to teach me, or one of these days I shall be wrecking you. You see there's always been a crew—'

'Crew!' – with sovereign contempt – 'why, the whole fun of the thing is to do everything oneself.'

'Well, I've felt in the way the whole morning.'

'I'm awfully sorry!' His dismay and repentance were comical. 'Why, it's just the other way; you may be all the use in the world.' He became absent.

We were following the inward trend of a small bay towards a cleft in the low shore.

'That's Ekken Sound,' said Davies; 'let's look into it,' and a minute or two later we were drifting through a dainty little strait, with a peep of open water at the end of it. Cottages bordered either side, some overhanging the very water, some connecting with it by a rickety wooden staircase or a miniature landing-stage. Creepers and roses rioted over the walls and tiny porches. For a space on one side, a rude quay with small smacks floating off it, spoke of some minute commercial interests; a very small tea-garden with neglected-looking bowers and leaf-strewn tables hinted at some equally minute tripping interest. A pervading hue of mingled bronze and rose came partly from the weather-mellowed woodwork of the cottages and stages, and partly from the creepers and the trees behind, where autumn's subtle fingers were already at work. Down this exquisite sea-lane we glided till it ended in a broad mere, where our sails which had been shivering and complaining filled into contented silence.

'Ready about!' said Davies callously. 'We must get out of this again,' and round we swung.

'Why not anchor and stop here?' I protested; for a view of tantalising loveliness was unfolding itself.

'Oh, we've seen all there is to be seen, and we must take this breeze while we've got it.' It was always torture to Davies to feel a good breeze running to waste while he was inactive at anchor or on shore. The 'shore' to him was an inferior element, merely serving as a useful annexe to the water – a source of necessary supplies.

'Let's have lunch,' he pursued, as we resumed our way down the fiord. A

vision of iced drinks, tempting salads, white napery, and an attentive stew-
ard mocked me with past recollections.

'You'll find a tongue,' said the voice of doom, 'in the starboard sofa-
locker; beer under the floor in the bilge. I'll see her round that buoy, if you
wouldn't mind beginning.' I obeyed with a bad grace, but the close air and
cramped posture must have benumbed my faculties, for I opened the port-
side locker, reached down and grasped a sticky body, which turned out to
be a pot of varnish. Recoiling wretchedly, I tried the opposite one, combat-
ing the embarrassing heel of the boat and the obstructive edges of the
centre-board case. A medley of damp tins of varied sizes showed in the
gloom, exuding a mouldy odour. Faded legends on dissolving paper, like
the remnants of old posters on a disused hoarding, spoke of soups, curries,
beefs, potted meats, and other hidden delicacies. I picked out a tongue, re-
imprisoned the odour, and explored for beer. It was true, I supposed, that
bilge didn't hurt it, as I tugged at the plank on my hands and knees, but I
should have myself preferred a more accessible and less humid wine-cellar
than the cavities among slimy ballast from which I dug the bottles. I
regarded my hard-won and ill-favoured pledges of a meal with giddiness
and discouragement.

'How are you getting on?' shouted Davies. 'The tin-opener's hanging up
on the bulkhead; the plates and knives are in the cupboard.'

I doggedly pursued my functions. The plates and knives met me half-
way, for being on the weather side, and thus having a downward slant, its
contents, when I slipped the latch, slid affectionately into my bosom and
overflowed with a clatter and jingle on to the floor.

'That often happens,' I heard from above. 'Never mind! There are no
breakables. I'm coming down to help.' And down he came, leaving the
Dulcibella to her own devices.

'I think I'll go on deck,' I said. 'Why in the world couldn't you lunch
comfortably at Ekken and save this infernal pandemonium of a picnic?
Where's the yacht going to meanwhile? And how are we to lunch on that
slanting table? I'm covered with varnish and mud, and ankle-deep in
crockery. There goes the beer!'

'You shouldn't have stood it on the table with this list on,' said Davies,
with intense composure, 'but it won't do any harm; it'll drain into the
bilge' (ashes to ashes, dust to dust, I thought). 'You go on deck now, and
I'll finish getting ready.' I regretted my explosion, though wrung from me
under great provocation.

'Keep her straight on as she's going,' said Davies, as I clambered up out
of the chaos, brushing the dust off my trousers and varnishing the ladder
with my hands. I unlashed the helm and kept her as she was going.

We had rounded a sharp bend in the fiord, and were sailing up a broad
and straight reach which every moment disclosed new beauties, sights fair
enough to be balm to the angriest spirit. A red-roofed hamlet was on our

left, on the right an ivied ruin, close to the water, where some contemplative cattle stood knee-deep. The view ahead was a white strand which fringed both shores, and to it fell wooded slopes, interrupted here and there by low sandstone cliffs of warm red colouring, and now and again by a dingle with cracks of green sward.

I forgot petty squalors and enjoyed things – the coy tremble of the tiller and the backwash of air from the dingy mainsail, and, with a somewhat chastened rapture, the lunch which Davies brought up to me and solicitously watched me eat.

Later, as the wind sank to lazy airs, he became busy with a larger topsail and jib; but I was content to doze away the afternoon drenching brain and body in the sweet and novel foreign atmosphere, and dreamily watching the fringe of glen, cliff and cool white sand as they passed ever more slowly by.

Through the Nukke Channel

Arthur Ransome
Racundra's First Cruise
first published 1928 (Mariners Library 1958)

*Arthur Ransome was much involved in the setting up of
the Mariners Library: he helped to select the titles, and
edited many of the volumes – several have forewords by
him. Unlike many others, his own contribution to the
series does not recount a voyage of outstanding achievement or hardship: it is simply the shake-down cruise
of a yacht that he had built to his own specification at
Riga on the Baltic. However, the author's feeling for
people, boats and the sea brings out the extraordinary in
everything. In this extract he describes an exhilarating
passage through a narrow channel. The 'Ancient
Mariner' referred to is the old man who crewed for
Ransome on* Racundra. *Readers of* Heavy Weather
Sailing *may be interested to know that* Racundra *and*
Annette II, *in which Adlard Coles and his wife
weathered a gale in the North Sea, are one and the same
yacht.*

I had left the lead overboard as a means of telling whether our anchor held, and three or four times in the night I went on deck to have a look at the lead-line. Once, when the wind had shifted and we had swung a quarter of a circle, the line stretching far out on our beam gave me a bit of a fright, but I went forward and found I could easily hold the boat by one hand on the chain. I took in the lead and dropped it again, and satisfied myself that we were not moving, and finally turned in so thoroughly reassured that I slept until six and was very unwilling to get up even then. However, the wind began to make a rowdy hullabaloo overhead, and at half-past six I turned out sleepily to find that it was blowing hard from the SE, dead against us.

I had been told that the channel was impossible for a sailing vessel against the wind and that the local sailors never attempt it, but wait at the entrance till the wind will take them through, this being the reason why yesterday we had met such a number of sail all together. Still, we had made our present anchorage against this same wind, and I decided to try to get through, making up my mind beforehand that there should be no false squeamishness about dropping back in case we should find ourselves engaged on a hopeless bit of work.

One can always find a good enough reason for doing anything that one has made up one's mind to do. In this case I had a perfect one, quite apart from the fact that we did not like staying where we were, and that the jam had been so good that we had eaten all the bread and could get no more till we should come to Hapsal. There was a reason *pro* and a reason *contra* – everything, in fact, that the human mind requires when it is putting up a pretence of being logical. The wind looked like continuing, but, so far as I could see through the long-distance glasses, there was not yet much current about the spar-buoys, which, however, were standing very high out of the water, tatters of seaweed clinging to them far above the waterline showing their more normal depth. I was sure of two things: the first, that a strong current would be setting against us out of the Sound within a very few hours, and the second, that I should have to deal with depths abnormally low. The first outweighed the second, and at seven in the morning our anchor was up and hanging at our bows, ready to drop at any moment in case of need, and we were off warily back to the fairway, the lead going all the time in two fathoms of water. Then we beat up towards the two spar-buoys that mark the entrance to the passage.

The men on a cutter whirling out of the channel with the wind behind them looked at us as if they thought we were mad and shrugged their shoulders with expression. But, though *Racundra* is not good at beating as compared with racing yachts, she is better against the wind than any of the local cutters and schooners, and, when we set her at it this morning, she seemed to know she was expected to do her best, and did it. There was a toughish wind, too, and that always suits her. With less wind we should not have tried it. At the same time, we left nothing to chance and took no risks of her missing stays, which, in this narrow way between rocks and sharply shoaling banks, would have meant almost inevitable disaster. I had sweated over the chart till I knew it pretty well by heart, and indeed only looked at it twice, and that when we were already through the actual channel and were out again in more or less open water, looking for the buoys and beacons that show the way into Hapsal Bay. I therefore set the Ancient at the tiller and went forward myself with the lead-line handy, though as a matter of fact there was never time to use it and it would have been useless, because there is no gradual shoaling. You are either in the channel with three fathoms of water or out of the channel with a fathom or less, or on a rock with no more than a couple of feet. My real business forward was to deal with the staysail in getting her quickly about and to con the little ship in without, if I could help it, communicating to the Ancient any of the doubts with which I was myself beset.

I kept my eyes on the sticks which here serve as spar-buoys, on the colour of the water and on the bottom, often only too visible, and shouted 'Ready about' in a tone as near as possible that in which those words are spoken when we are at sea and have the whole Baltic to make mistakes in. At first the Ancient was just a little bit petulant at the frequency of our tacks, but we touched once with the centreboard from hanging on an extra second, once only, and from that moment he was perfect and everything worked in the delirious, exciting manner of tight-rope walking. He knew then that we really were on a tight-rope, and that this was not an example of my ridiculous preference for imagining, when navigating, that *Racundra* has the draught of a big ship. We swung round as the words were out of my mouth; I had the staysail aback till the mainsail filled, and we were off again, rushing from side to side of the channel, making a bit every time, creeping up in hurried zigzags, a dozen or so between each buoy. The chart that I had read so often in the winter took visible solid shape as we moved. There was Mereholm; there those rocks awash; there two windmills on Nukke; there, at last, the buoy with a ball and two brooms, bases apart, on the top. The brooms are not there, but that must be the buoy none the less.

It is hard enough to give an idea of how things looked. At first, of course, there was the open sea behind us, and we were pushing our way in between the wooded island of Worms and the low, grass-patched and rocky main-land. The two were always a good distance apart, but outcrops from both of them were close to us either above or under water, and at times it was difficult to preserve one's faith in chart knowledge and to sail so near those brown rocks with such a space of open water on the other side. How much simpler to sail boldly up the middle. And then, on the other tack, just a few score yards, often less, and there were more rocks under the water, or pale green shallows splashed with dark, and we were thankfully about again and scuttling back towards the brown lumps that at least were out of water and less secretive in their villainy. And yet, what a stretch of water! and round *Racundra* would go again, the wavelets foaming under her bows, and so on, to and fro, to and fro, each time gaining a little southwards against the wind, through gusts of which I had to yell to be heard by the Ancient at the tiller.

I had enjoyed following the intricate Moon Sound channel from Paternoster through by the Erik Stone and Harry Island to the open sea, but there big ships could go, and we had a margin of yards and sometimes far more, in case we left it for a moment. Here there was no margin at all. We were ourselves drawing with centreboard down (as we had to have it down for beating against the wind) more than most of the small coasters who alone use this channel. It was incredibly exciting, the more so that as we proceeded, and time went on and the wind still blew, there was visibly growing current against us from the S through the channel. It became a race between us and the current and the wind. Could we get through to the open and round into the bay of Hapsal before the wind had made the current so great that we could not hold against it? Each spar-buoy left astern was a separate triumph, and I would hardly let myself believe that we had left the worst of the channel behind us until the view before us had already widened, and we could see far into the broad Sound, where hull-down were three goose-winged schooners hurrying from the S before the wind that for them was a friendly ally, the same wind that *Racundra*, sailing from the N, had had to meet and conquer. Now, after just four hours of frenzied beating, we were making longer tacks, keeping our eyes on two tall beacons on the mainland on the southern side of Hapsal Bay, already within the mouth of the inlet, and watching to bring two other beacons in line under Hapsal town with its church and ruined castle. Those two beacons, one on shore and one on a bit of a rock almost awash, would lead us safely between the shallows towards the little Hapsal harbour, on the quay of which again are two other beacons, which, taken in line, help little ships through the last few hundred yards of their passage. We shifted from the line of the first pair to the line of the second, found the spar-buoys that supplement these land signs, and then, sailing E with the wind free, fairly foamed from buoy to buoy until at noon we rounded up and anchored beside two small trading cutters about a cable's length from Hapsal pierhead.

Storm in the Southern Ocean

Eric Newby
The Last Grain Race
first published 1956 (Mariners Library 1968)

Eric Newby may be unique in having left a job in an advertising agency to sail in a grain clipper. He did this in 1938, and sailed in Moshulu, *owned by Gustaf Erikson, the last large scale operator of clipper ships. Newby's account of the round trip to Australia is full of the wry humour which the crew share in their unequal battle against the elements. Here he describes the most awe-inspiring part of the voyage, a storm encountered when the ship was two weeks out from Australia.*

I glanced at the barometer. It had been falling steadily since 4 o'clock on Wednesday morning, the 22nd. On that day, except for some light north-erly airs, we had been becalmed on a sea as grey and unvarying as a featureless plain. The albatross had vanished. At midnight on Wednesday the wind had been a gentle breeze from the NW and by the afternoon of Thursday, the 23rd, *Moshulu* was logging 12 knots with a WNW wind, force 5. At 8 it had shifted to the west, the yards were squared, the spankers and the gaff topsail were taken in and she ran before it. The time was now 4 p.m. on the 24th, the wind WSW. The air was full of masses of white and grey cloud moving rapidly eastward above the ship, which was being driven and lifted forward with a slight see-saw motion on the crest of seas of immense depth and power. These seas did not seem to be raised by wind; instead they seemed the product of some widespread underwater convulsion. All round the ship the sea was surging and hurling itself into the air in plumes of spray, occasionally leaping over the rail by the mizzen braces and filling the main deck with a swirl of white water. The air was bitter; I could see Tria's breath smoking.

'It looks all right to me,' I said.

'I don' say right now,' said Tria. 'But very soon this bloddy ting gets so much as she can stand. Lissun when you go aloft.'

We were joined by the Sailmaker, who stood for some time looking up at the main royal with the wind straining in it, then over the rail at the mounting sea. 'Going to blow,' he said.

Hilbert came racing down the deck from the 'Vaskrum' forrard, dressed in nothing but wooden clogs and fresh long underwear, his teeth chatter-ing. All he said was: 'Vind,' and vanished into the starboard fo'c'sle. The First Mate looked down at us from the midship deck. 'Going to vind a little too mooch,' he began conversationally.

'For Christ's sake,' I said, rather too audibly.

'What the hell are you doing?' he demanded, noticing me.

'Backstern, Sir.'

'Backstern doesn't take all bloddy day. Get down in the hold with babord'svakt for knacka rost.'

I went below to where the port watch were working suspended on plat-forms over one of the 'tween-deck hatches. The only vacant space was next to Taanila, even more gnomelike than usual in goggles. I slipped in beside him and he turned as the platform gave a lurch. 'I tink . . .' he began. In that moment I wondered exactly what he was going to think. Was he going to think that I needed a knife inserted in some delicate part? Was he going to remind me yet again of my unfortunate nationality? Or was he going to tell me his opinion of 'knacka rost'?

'I tink it is going to . . .'

'Don't tell me, let me guess – to vind.'

'Yo, yo. How you know?'

'Because I'm bloody clever.'

At 5 the heavy chain sheet to the fore royal parted on the port side. We just managed to get the sail in before it blew itself to pieces. The remaining royals had to come in, and the flying jib, then all hands went aloft for the main and mizzen courses. All through the night there were two helmsmen. The wind increased and the seas rose higher and began to pour into the ship again. In the watch below I lay awake listening to the clang of freeing ports along the length of the main deck as they opened to the pressure of water and closed as the ship rolled away, tipping the sea right across her so that the same process took place on the other side. With more apprehension I listened to the sound of water trickling steadily into the fo'c'sle through a cracked port above Bäckmann's bunk. This seemed to constitute a far greater threat to our comfort than the more spectacular effects outside.

At 5.30 on the morning of the second Friday, *Moshulu*, still carrying her upper topgallants, began to labour under the onslaught of the heavy seas which were flooding on to the deck like a mill race. It was quite dark as six of us clewed-up the mizzen lower topgallant, and although from where I was at the tail of the rope I could see nothing at all except the hunched shoulders of Jansson ahead of me, I could hear Tria at the head of the line exhorting us. The sail was almost up when the wind fell quite suddenly and we all knew that we were in the trough of a wave far bigger than anything we had yet experienced. It was far too dark to see it at a distance, we could only sense its coming as the ship rolled slightly to port to meet it.

'Hoold . . .' someone began to shout as the darkness became darker still and the sea came looming over the rail. I was end man. There was just time to take a turn with the clewline round my middle and a good hold, the next moment it was on top of us. The rope was not torn from me; instead it was as though a gentle giant had smoothed his hands over my knuckles. They simply opened of their own accord and I unravelled from it like a cotton reel from the end of a thread and was swept away. As I went another body bumped me, and I received a blow in the eye from a seaboot. Then I was alone, rushing onwards and turning over and over. My head was filled with bright lights like a by-pass at night, and the air was full of the sounds of a large orchestra playing out of tune. In spite of this there was time to think and I thought: 'I'm done for.' At the same time the words of a sea poem, 'ten men hauling the lee fore brace . . . seven when she rose at last', came back to me with peculiar aptness. But only for an instant because now I was turning full somersaults, hitting myself violently again and again as I met something flat which might have been the coaming of No. 4 hatch, or the top of the charthouse, for all I knew. Then I was over it, full of water and very frightened, thinking 'Is this what it's like to drown?' No more obstructions now but still going very fast and still under water, perhaps no longer in the ship, washed overboard, alone in the Southern Ocean. Quite suddenly there was a parting of water, a terrific crash as my head hit something solid, and I felt myself aground.

Finding myself in the lee scuppers with my head forced right through a freeing port so that the last of the great sea behind me spurted about my ears, I was in a panic that a second wave might come aboard and squeeze me through it like a sausage, to finish me off.

Staggering to my feet, my oilskins ballooning with water, too stupid from the blow on my head to be frightened, I had just enough sense to jump for the starboard lifeline when the next wave came boiling over the port quarter and obliterated everything from view.

Swinging above the deck on the lifeline with the sea sucking greedily at my seaboots, I began to realise what a fortunate escape I had had from serious injury, for the alacrity with which I had leapt for the lifeline in spite of the great weight of sea-water inside my oilskins had convinced me that I had suffered no damage except the bang on the head.

The sea had taken me and swept me from the pin rail of the mizzen rigging, where I had been working, diagonally across the deck for fifty feet past the Jarvis brace winches, on the long handles of which I could so easily have been speared, over the fife rails of the mizzen mast, right over the top of No. 3 hatch and into the scuppers by the main braces outside the Captain's quarters.

'Where you bin?' demanded Tria accusingly, when I managed to join the little knot of survivors who were forcing their way waist deep across the deck, spluttering, cursing, and spitting sea-water as they came.

'Paddling,' I said, relieved to find that there were still six of us.

'Orlright, don' be all bloody day,' he added unsympathetically. 'Tag i gigtåget. One more now. Ooh – ah, oh, bräck dem.'

'What happened?' I asked Jansson.

'That goddam Valker let her come up too mooch,' said Jansson. 'I bin all over the bloddy deck in that sea.'

On the second Friday *Moshulu's* noon position was 50° 19′ 4 S, 170° 36′ 9 W. In 23½ hours she had sailed 296 miles. This was the best day's sailing with cargo she ever had with Erikson. It was only bettered by the Germans on very few occasions. Twice in 1909 on a voyage from Newcastle, NSW, to Valparaiso when loaded with nearly 5,000 tons of coal she ran 300 miles.

At midnight the wind was SW, force 6, and in the early hours of Saturday morning I went aloft with Hermansonn in a storm of sleet to make fast the main upper topgallant. It was now blowing a fresh gale, force 8, and the yard was swinging like a mad thing; we had a terrible time with this sail. Some of the gaskets had been caught in the buntline blocks on the yard and were immovable, others were missing. The sleet numbed our fingers until we almost cried with cold.

Below us, in the fore and mizzen rigging, eight boys were having the time of their lives furling the lower topgallants; on the mizzen two buntlines had carried away to starboard and the sail was being clewed-up to the yard with lines taken to the capstan on the main deck, where from time to time ton upon ton of white water poured over the rail, causing those heaving at the capstan bars to abandon their efforts and leap for the lifelines.

'OOH, what bloddy cold,' screamed Hermansonn. 'Ut, Kossuri, you strongbody, you rosbif, ut, ut, på nock.'

As we reached the yardarm there was a great ripping sound that seemed to come from below, and we both hung dizzily over the yard to see whether the upper topsail had blown out. Then, in spite of the wind and our precarious situation, Hermansonn began to laugh. I knew then that I had suffered some dire misfortune as Hermansonn only laughed in that way when a disaster happened to someone else.

'Ho, ho!' he boomed above the gale, 'Ho, ho, focking fonny!'

'What?' I screamed in his ear. 'Tell me.'

'Your trousers, ho, ho, English, no good.'

It was true. My oilskin trousers, unable to stand the strain to which they had been subjected, had split from end to end.

This was an accident of the worst kind. To find myself half way across the Southern Ocean, in the stormiest seas in the world, with defective oilskin trousers, was calamity.

By the time I had mended the trousers, the free watch was nearly over. I was 'Backstern', and having made sure that Kroner had put on the washing-up water, I waited for a lull to dash forward to the fo'c'sle head from where I could look back along the ship.

Moshulu was running ten knots in the biggest seas I had ever seen. As I watched, the poop began to sink before my eyes and the horizon astern was blotted out by a high polished wall, solid and impenetrable like marble. The poop went on dropping until the whole ship seemed to be toppling backwards into the deep moat below the wall of water that loomed over her, down and down to the bottom of the sea itself. At the moment when it seemed that this impregnable mass must engulf us, a rift appeared in its face and it collapsed, burrowing beneath the ship, bearing her up so that what a moment before seemed a sluggish, solid hulk destined for the sea bed was now like a bird skimming the water, supported by the wind high above the valley.

This was noon.

In the first part of the afternoon the barometer was low, 742 millimetres. At one moment *Moshulu* would be riding the crests in brilliant sunshine, the next swooping down a great incline of water peppered by rain and hailstones, yawing a little from her course and beginning to roll, taking sea as high as her charthouse. Everyone was soaking wet and none of us had any more dry clothes. Everything in the Vuitton was wet as well. All through the afternoon we were kept busy making new wire buntlines, cold work with no movement in it, but by coffee-time one of my shirts had dried over the galley fire and I put it on rejoicing. But not for long.

As soon as I came out on deck I heard the captain's voice.

'We'll see what she can stand,' he said, looking aloft in a speculative way like a gambler about to stake a large sum on an uncertainty.

'Aloft and break out the main lower topgallant. Lively now.' As I went I heard Sedelquist, who had been at the wheel with me, say: 'Crazy focker.' Privately agreeing with him, I swung myself on to the pin rail and into the main rigging. Aloft the wind seemed as strong as ever, and I looked down to a deck as narrow as a ruler on which the tiny figures of the watch were clustered, waiting to perform the ticklish job of sheeting home the sail which I was about to loose from its gaskets.

A distant cry borne on the wind told me that they were ready.

I cast off the gaskets on the weather side, hauled up a good slack on the buntlines and, scuttling into the rigging, clung to the shrouds for my life. The yard began to plunge and whip, the buntlines plucked at the blocks seized to the shrouds, making the ratlines tremble underfoot.

'She'll never stand it,' was the general verdict when I regained the deck.

With the sail sheeted home there was too much strain on the entire sail structure and at eight o'clock the upper topsail sheet carried away and the sail had to be taken in, together with the lower topgallant we had recently set.

Thus reduced, we drove on in the darkness with both topsails set on the fore and mizzen, the main lower topsail, the foresail and one fore-and-aft sail – the jigger staysail.

This was the night of the second Friday, March 24th. We were wet and fed up and though we cursed *Moshulu* and the Captain too, we were pleased with him for pushing her to the limit.

'This Kapten is proper strongbody for vind,' said Sandell after an issue of rum and a good dinner of Lobscouse – a sustaining hash made from pounded hard biscuit, potato and 'Buffelo'.

'—— the Kapten,' replied Sedelquist who was absolutely cynical about all men. 'Vonts to get his name in the papers, I shouldn't vonder.'

'We'll be in it too, if he does,' I said.

'Yes, in the bloddy paper but on the front with beeg black lines all round "missing". That's what we'll be.'

It was too cold to argue. I slipped into my bunk dressed in my soaking long underwear with two pullovers on top. On my head was a very hairy balaclava helmet, so that I looked like the subject of some hitherto unpublished photograph of a military man in the lines about Sebastopol.

Just before midnight the voice of the 'påpass' woke me. My long underwear was steaming like a kettle. Outside it was fearfully cold. Because it was my 'utkik' I put on as many layers as I could: a wet hairy shirt and trousers that I had bought in the East India Dock Road, two more pullovers in addition to the two I was sleeping in, and my heavy pilot coat. Everything was dripping with water.

'Remember *Admiral Karpfanger* – keep good "utkik", plenty ice around here, maybe,' screamed Tria cheerfully in my ear, and left me.

At the lookout I peered ahead of the ship and could see nothing. The air was full of spray which rose like mist about the ship. The wind was strong enough to lean on. High above in the darkness the rest of the watch was bending a fresh chain-sheet for the main upper topsail.

With the new sheet bent we started to wind the yard into position. The gearing on the winch was very low and it was a slow job to raise it. By three in the morning it was in position and we had set the sail, together with the main lower topgallant which the Captain was determined she should carry.

But it was no use. The barometer continued to fall, and at five the starboard watch had to furl it again. This was on the morning of March 25th.

'Going to blow, I tink,' said Tria.

'What do you think it's doing now?' I asked him.

'Notting.'

'Golly.'

After breakfast I was at 'Backstern', extremely bad-tempered because I had been washed away when crossing the foredeck to the starboard fo'c'sle and had lost all the hot water.

Suddenly Taanila appeared. 'Kom,' he said.

'Why? I'm "Backstern".'

'Styrman, he say "BRÄCK GÅRDINGARNA PÅ STOR ÖVRE MÄRS".'

'This is it,' said Kroner as I went aft. 'Upper topsails. It's going to be really big.'

'It's the blasted "Backstern" that worries me. There's no water.'

'I'll put some on for you,' he answered. 'It'll be there when you come back.'

'Maybe I shan't,' I said, nearer the mark than usual.

When we were all assembled the Mate slacked away the hand brake of the upper topsail halliard winch and set it spinning. The eighty-foot yard began to descend in its greased track on the fore part of the mizzen mast, and as the weather sheet was progressively eased we clewed-up to windward and manned the buntlines. With the weather clew up, the lee side was easier and the sail was furled without incident.

The fore upper topsail was the most difficult. All the buntlines jammed and more than half the robands securing the sail to the jackstay had gone. The outer buntline block had broken loose and was flailing in the air, so that when we reached the lowered yard eighty feet above the sea, we hesitated a moment before the 'Horry ops' of the Mates behind us drove us out on to the footropes, hesitated because the bunt of the sail was beating back over the yard. The wind was immense. It no longer blew in the accepted sense of the word at all; instead it seemed to be tearing apart the very substance of the atmosphere. Nor was the sound of it any longer definable in ordinary terms. It no longer roared, screamed, sobbed or sang according to the various levels on which it was encountered. The power and noise of this wind was now more vast and all-comprehending, in its way as big as the sky, bigger than the sea itself, making something that the mind baulked at, so that it took refuge in blankness.

It was in this negative state of mind that could accept anything without qualm, even the possibility of death, that I fell off the yard backwards. I was the last man out on the weather side and was engaged in casting loose a gasket before we started to work on the sail, when without warning it flicked up, half the foot of a topsail, 40 feet of canvas as hard as corrugated iron, and knocked me clean off the footrope.

There was no interval for reflection, no sudden upsurge of remorse for past sins, nor did my life pass in rapid review before my eyes. Instead there was a delightful jerk and I found myself entangled in the weather rigging some five feet below the yard, and as soon as I could I climbed back to the yard and carried on with my job. I felt no fear at all until much later on.

It needed three-quarters of an hour to make fast the weather side. Time and time again we nearly had the sail to the yard when the wind tore it from our fingers.

My companion aloft was Alvar.

'What happened?' he said when we reached the deck.

'I fell.'

'I din' see,' he said in a disappointed way. 'I don' believe.'

'I'm damned if I'm going to do it again just because you didn't see it.'

'I don' believe.'

'Orlright,' I said. 'The next time I'll tell you when I'm going to fall off.'

'Dot's bettair,' said Alvar.

At noon on Saturday, the 25th, our position was 50° 7′ S, 164° 21′ W. In the 23½ hours from noon on the 24th *Moshulu* had sailed 241 miles and made 228 between observed positions. Her previous day's runs were 296 and 282, but the violence of the sea and the necessary reduction in canvas were slowing her increasingly.

The barometer fell and fell, 746, 742, 737 millimetres. The sun went down astern, shedding a pale watery yellow light on the undersides of the deep black clouds hurrying above the ship. It was extremely cold, colder than it had ever been, blowing a strong gale, force 9. Big seas were coming aboard. I felt very lonely. The ship that had seemed huge and powerful was nothing now, a speck in the Great Southern Ocean, two thousand miles eastwards of New Zealand, three thousand from the coast of South America, separated to the North from the nearest inhabited land, the Cook Islands and Tahiti, by two thousand miles of open sea; to the South there was nothing but the Antarctic ice and darkness. She was running before seas that were being generated in the greatest expanse of open ocean, of a power and size unparalleled because there was no impediment to them as they drove eastwards round the world. She was made pygmy too by the wind, the wind that was already indescribable, that Tria said had only now begun to blow.

At this moment, for the first time I felt certain of the existence of an infinitely powerful and at the same time merciful God. Nearly everyone in the ship felt something of this, no one spoke of it. We were all of us awed by what we saw and heard beyond the common experience of men.

I had second wheel in the watch till midnight with Jansson to help me. We relieved Yonny Valker and Bäckmann.

'Törn om,' I said, mounting the platform next to Yonny and feeling with my foot for the brake pedal.

'Törn om,' repeated Yonny, showing me that he was ready to be relieved.

'Othtnordotht,' he lisped, giving me the course (we were running before the storm ENE), and then added as he relinquished the wheel: 'No more babords.'

It seemed reasonable. The ship was pointing ENE½E, but with the rolling it was difficult to keep her right on course and I supposed that he had already given her as much port helm as she needed.

I was soon disillusioned. Yonny had left me with the wheel hard to starboard and she continued to run off in that direction.

Before Tria awoke to what was happening *Moshulu* was pointing south east. Unfortunately he lost his head; shrieking wildly, he began to turn the binnacle hood towards Jansson so that he could see the card, but only turned the hood sufficiently for the card to be invisible to both of us. At this moment the First Mate arrived and, thinking Jansson was at fault, began to give him hell. Not even the fact that I was standing on the weather side convinced him that I was helmsman.

It needed the four of us to return the ship to her course, and she took some terrific seas aboard. Afterwards the Mate laid into Jansson until the latter's nose began to glow red.

'It was my fault,' I shouted, trying to make my voice heard above the wind.

'Shot op, shot op!' bellowed the Mate with such violence that I dared not say another word. 'Shot op, or by *helvete* be jus' too bloddy bad.'

I shut up.

'I'm sorry,' I said to Jansson afterwards.

'Orlright,' he said, 'not dead, but nearly. We'll make some cocoa in the "Doonkey Hus".'

As the barometer went on falling, the wind rose. At 4 a.m. it fell to 733 metres and the wind blew force 10, Beaufort notation, a whole gale of wind. The starboard watch took in the main upper topsail at three o'clock and the ship ran before the storm under lower topsails and the foresail; the whole of the after deck was inundated.

'A liddle more,' said Sandell, 'she'll take a liddle more than this.'

Day broke at last, slowly because clouds, black as night, pressed upon the ship. Hail, driving rain and flurries of snow fell. At five the watch was called. We knew the reason before the Mate gave the order.

'Undra märs skot,' said Sedelquist. 'Got to slack those lower topsail sheets before it's too late.'

The main deck was like a reef with occasionally the tops of the winches and the hatches breaking the surface, and it seemed strange to me that a week ago, when we had been securing the hatch covers with heavy timbers, the precautions had seemed superfluous, almost too adequate, and yet now I found myself wondering what would happen if one of those awful cliff-like seas caught up with the ship and pooped her.

On the deck we were caught in a roaring flood and jumped for the lifelines, hanging on minutes at a time, but with her topsails eased she ran better and there was less danger of the sail blowing out.

At six o'clock, cold yet exultant, we went below for coffee.

'She's a real ship,' said Sandell. 'I've never seen a ship like this. Blows like strongbody. Mos' ships you'd have the foresail off her and heave-to. Lovs vind, lovs it. But my God if ve have to take the foresail, be someting.'

The clouds cleared and a whole gale of wind blew out of a clear blue sky. At eight the wind reached its greatest velocity, force 11 on the Beaufort scale, a wind in which a wooden ship might well have foundered, and a lesser than *Moshulu* would have hove to, drifting to leeward, lying on the wind under a storm trysail.

All through the storm the pigs had been setting up despairing cries, as well they might, cooped in their narrow steel coffins. At six o'clock we cleaned out their sties, a difficult job in a ship running before a great gale. It took three of us to do it.

'For Chrissake don' let them go,' grunted Tria, as we levered the iron troughs through the door of the sty with crowbars.

He had no sooner said this than Auguste and Filimon, believing that the ship was about to founder, charged the barricade of hatch covers with which we had fenced them in, intent on finding a place in the boats. The barricade collapsed and Filimon, who was leading, shot between Tria's legs, upsetting him in the nasty mess we were shovelling up. Auguste followed him closely, and they both went glissading away on their behinds into the lee scuppers, from which we had difficulty in rescuing them.

'Better eat them before they go overside,' I said as we struggled with Auguste, who was threshing about under water.

'I don' care how soon we eat that Filimon,' Tria said.

Moshulu continued to carry her sail and the storm entered its last and most impressive phase. We were cold and wet and yet too excited to sleep. Some stood on the fo'c'sle head but only for a short time as the force of the wind made it difficult to remain on two feet. Others stood beneath it and gazed out along the ship, watching the seas rearing up astern as high as a three-storeyed house. It was not only their height that was impressive but their length. Between the greatest of them there was a distance that could only be estimated in relation to the ship, as much as four times her entire length, or nearly a quarter of a mile. The seas approached very deliberately, black and shiny as jet, with smoking white crests gleaming in the sunshine, hissing as they came, hurling a fine spume into the air as high as the main yard.

I went aloft in the fore rigging, out of the comparative shelter of the foresail, into the top, and higher again to the cross-trees, where I braced myself to the backstays. At this height, 130 feet up, in a wind blowing 70 miles an hour, the noise was an unearthly scream. Above me was the naked topgallant yard and above that again the royal to which I presently climbed. I was now used to heights but the bare yard, gleaming yellow in the sunshine, was groaning and creaking on its tracks. The high whistle of the wind through the halliards sheaf, and above all the pale blue illimitable sky, cold and serene, made me deeply afraid and conscious of my insignificance.

Far below, the ship was an impressive sight. For a time the whole of the after deck would disappear, hatches, winches, everything, as the solid water hit it, and then, like an animal pulled down by hounds, she would rise and shake them from her, would come lifting out of the sea with her freeing ports spouting.

Opening my camera, I attached the lens hood, but the wind blew it into the sea. The mist of spray rising all about the ship made it almost impossible to see anything through the viewfinder. There was no need for the range-finder. I simply set the scale to infinity and pressed the button, and even that was difficult enough.

Later, I was standing on deck just aft of the charthouse when a monster wave reared over the main rail and exploded on the house itself. As it came I shut the camera but was too late to shut the case.

In an agony of mind I went down to the fo'c'sle. The camera was very wet. The film was undamaged. I upended it and a thin trickle of water ran out of the Compur shutter. The rest of the watch were observing me with interest.

'I'll have to take it to pieces or it'll rust up,' I explained.

'Good,' said everybody. 'Now.'

'No, when the storm finishes. The thing's full of springs.'

'Put it in the offen,' said Sedelquist. 'I should ask the "Kock". Dry heem out.'

By noon *Moshulu* had again run 228 miles. Since the storm began we had crossed 18 degrees of longitude. Now the barometer rose steadily. The starboard watch reset the fore and main upper topsails and all through the afternoon we were resetting sail. Big seas were still coming aboard and we frequently deserted the halliard winches for the lifelines. Sent aloft to overhaul the buntlines, I returned in a filthy temper because I had dropped my knife overboard.

By 9 p.m. the gale had passed, the wind had fallen but there was still a tremendous sea running. The weather was clear and cold with overhead a thin crescent moon. At two in the morning of Monday, the 27th, we reset the main royal and in an hour or two more we were in full sail again.

From the Log of Vertue XXXV

Humphrey Barton
Vertue XXXV
first published 1950 (Mariners Library 1955)

*In 1950, Humphrey Barton sailed a 25-foot Vertue class
sloop across the Atlantic with one crew, Kevin O'Riordan
(referred to as K. O'R in the extracts). The passage was
marked by numerous gales and a final storm which nearly
proved disastrous when a wave broke on top of the boat,
damaging the cabin structure severely. His log of the voyage blends narrative of day to day events with detailed
accounts of shipboard life, and reflection on the whole
business of sailing small boats across oceans. The author,
recently awarded the Blue Water Medal by the Cruising
Club of America, writes:*

'There were two main reasons why I made the voyage
across the North Atlantic in the 25-foot engineless sloop,
Vertue XXXV.

'Firstly, I had been invited by the owner of the nearly
new 55-foot ocean racing yacht, Gulvain, which he had
entered for the Bermuda and Transatlantic Races, to be
her sailing master, but he was shipping her across.
Therefore I had to find a means of getting myself to the
other side.

'Secondly, I wanted to prove that a small engineless
yacht could battle her way against the prevailing westerly
wind, as lack of time prevented me from taking the trade
wind route, which would have doubled the distance from
Falmouth to New York. I was already intensely interested in the history of small boat crossings of the
N. Atlantic, and this led me, some years later, to write
another book, entitled Atlantic Adventurers.'

The Dangers of Ocean Voyaging

We really are becalmed now and I have lowered the genoa. I could hang up a light and turn in, but both K. O'R and I are agreed that it is really wiser for the man on watch to remain up. Then if a light air comes along he can get the yacht going again at once; and in the unlikely event of a ship or a squall approaching he can deal with the situation. If one were all alone, it would be a very different matter, of course, and one would immediately take advantage of a calm to catch up on sleep. But K. O'R and I are getting all the sleep we need these days.

How I admire the fellows who do these tremendous voyages all alone. What courage, endurance and confidence in themselves and their little ships they must have. It is so much easier to be brave when with someone else, than when all alone.

I often wonder just what are the risks of this voyaging in very small yachts. That they are extremely slight is proved by the very, very small number of yachts which have disappeared without trace; I can think of only three, of which Slocum's *Spray* was one. The greatest risk is, I think, the freak wave which just falls upon a small yacht with devastating force and smashes up her deckworks; but the freak wave is probably the product of a freak gale. Minor negligible risks are lightning, fire and collision. Severe illness of the crew, such as might be caused by food poisoning, is always a possibility. Irving Johnson with his big schooner *Yankee* very nearly got into serious difficulty in the South Pacific from just such a cause. If a main fresh-water tank sprang a leak and ran dry, one might be in a bit of a jamb, but the wise owner does not keep all his eggs in the one basket.

In bad weather there is a great risk of falling overboard, or being washed overboard, and I am very strongly of the opinion that every sea-going yacht should have lifelines all round. They not only add enormously to the safety of everyone aboard but the crew can get about so much more quickly. They know that if they should slip, fall or lose their balance the lifelines will save them. Two lines are better than one and the upper should be thirty inches above the deck, not an inch less. Rope is useless; the ideal is three-quarter-inch circumference stainless-steel wire. Stanchions should be of galvanized mild steel tube one and a quarter inches diameter, or tapered light alloy tubes, such as I have in *Vertue XXXV*. The sockets should be fastened to both rail and covering board and, if possible, there should be a nut and screw bolt fastening right through to the shelf.

I can think of several chaps who would be alive now if their yachts had been fitted with lifelines and stanchions. A pulpit is well worth having in yachts with forestays to the stem head. They are not really necessary, I think, when the forestay is well inboard, as there is then no need for a man to go right forward.

One of the major problems in any small yacht is to keep the water out of her in bad weather. She may be as tight as a bottle in normal conditions but as soon as she gets into really bad weather the sea finds its way below. The main causes seem to be leaking hatches, skylights, portlights, naval pipe and, of course, the cockpit. Most of these leaks can be eliminated. The forehatch must either have a waterproof cover or be of the screw-down type. The companionway hatch, when open, should be completely enclosed by a light wood casing. The flush-fitting type of forehatch in the for'ard end of the modern straight-through coach roof invariably leaks very badly. The hatch with the double coaming is said to be good, but I have never tried it. Skylights require very careful designing and must have waterproof covers. Portlights can be absolutely tight, provided that the rubber washers are not perished nor the frames strained. A leaking port-light can often be made tight by the judicious use of a spanner on the wing nut. Naval pipes are rather a problem. In *Vertue XXXV* I did not have one fitted, but I am carrying it with me for the next owner to fit. I have tried stuffing them up with greasy rags but I think that the real solution is to unshackle the anchor cable and plug the hole from underneath with a large cork.

The cockpit remains a problem in small yachts. It is very easy to make it watertight up to seat level, as in *Vertue XXXV*, and it may be thought that that is good enough. But it is simply astonishing the amount of water that found its way under the lids of the seats during the earlier part of this voyage. In bad weather the sea pours in over the lee coamings, and as the yacht is invariably heeled well down in such conditions, little of it finds its way into the cockpit. Instead it lies down to leeward in the angle formed by seat and coamings. I have a small drain at the forward end on each side to carry water through to the cockpit, but it is quite inadequate to deal with large quantities. I admit that these drains should have been very much larger but, even so, quite a lot of water would still have found its way under the lifting seat tops and thence to the bilge.

I toyed with the idea of carrying the cockpit floor right out to the ship's side, but I would have lost a great deal of locker space and I would have increased enormously the potential quantity of sea that could flood that part of the yacht. To have fixed tops to the seats would be unthinkable, as one would lose so much valuable storage space, and this space is very inaccessible from the accommodation. In the seat lockers and after locker we stow three warps, four fenders, Nos. 2 and 3 staysails, spinnaker gear, spare sheets, a small sea anchor, bosun's chair, a four-gallon water-can, water funnel, companionway washboards, two tins of flares, log box, cock-pit cushions, anchor buoy, spare light alloy stanchion, reefing gear, two lifejackets and the bellows for the dinghy. Yet there is room for more.

Maintaining Standards

We have so far remained reasonably civilized but I for one am slowly but inevitably deteriorating over small matters. I used, for instance, to fold up neatly my sleeping bag and eiderdown and stow them properly in the recess at the end of my bunk. Now I just kick them all in higgledy-piggledy down into the recess, pushing them well home with my feet, throw in a garment or two after them, stuff in my bolster (half the International Code of flags) and bung up the entrance to the cavern with my pillow. The latter, having been stripped of its white cover, serves as a cushion by day. K. O'R still folds up all his bedding, but then he is a better man than I am, Gungha Din. I even use my egg-spoon to stir my tea with now.

Fear

I have just been up into the cockpit to have a look round. It is a lovely warm, starlight night and it is difficult to believe that any bad weather can be on the way. Oh, well, if it does come we can face it. We know the drill pretty well by now. But I do hope we do not get as severe a gale as the last one. Not that I had any doubt as to the ability of the yacht to come through that blow safely, but there is always the horrid thought at the back of one's mind that a gale may turn out to be a freak storm with winds going up to 80 m.p.h. or more, with seas forty feet high and crests of four or five feet. Would the yacht come safely through those conditions? I do not know. I think she probably would but one cannot be certain. What a cursed thing a vivid imagination is. And what a still more cursed thing fear is. One is afraid of the unknown. Afraid of what might happen. Afraid of death, of course; and very naturally so. I would not like to drown and I have no intention of drowning. I am determined to get this yacht, and K. O'R and myself safely to New York, come what may, but by Heaven! I shall be glad when we get there.

I must be slightly depressed this evening. I will think about Shackleton's famous voyage in the boat *James Caird* from Elephant Island to South Georgia across 600 miles of one of the stormiest oceans of the world. They had appalling weather and bitter cold the whole way: an epic voyage if ever there was one. They came safely through weather far worse than any we are likely to encounter in a far less seaworthy craft. So whatever have I got to worry about? Nothing at all.

Waking Up for a Night Watch

In *Vertue XXXV* the twin clock and barometer is fastened to the forward coaming of the doghouse. This coaming is raked aft slightly, and I find when lying in my bunk that I can just get a fore-shortened view of the hands and so tell the time.

I have got into the habit of waking up towards the end of my watch below. Tonight I awoke at a quarter to twelve. In another ten minutes I shall hear K. O'R in his gruff old voice say: 'Twelve o'clock.' I am completely awake and refreshed after three and a half hours' deep, peaceful sleep. I lie listening carefully. Above me the genoa sheet creaks incessantly in its lead. There is a distant familiar rattle which I know to be the topping lift shackle at the boom end. A dull, hollow thump for'ard tells me that the genoa is falling in. From that I deduce that either the wind is very light or that it is so far aft that the sail is being blanketed behind the mainsail, probably the latter, as the cabin lamp flickers occasionally, and it only does that when the wind is abaft the beam. The movement of the yacht is slight but erratic, and as I lie on my back gazing at the deckhead above I can feel my body move gently from side to side. In a sudden moment of energy I reach up and let go the two after lashings of the canvas lee guard. At the same time I take another upward glance at the clock. Only ten to twelve: I have another five minutes. Why turn out yet? I flop back on to my pillow. My thoughts flicker back 2,000 miles and next moment I am fast asleep again.

'Twelve o'clock,' says a far-distant voice.

I produce a ghastly sort of groan to let him know that I am awake but not feeling at my best as yet.

'What about a time signal?' he asks.

I click down the switch of the radio set and instantly a brass band tears the quiet night to pieces with distorted music. In the background a man is talking monotonously and rapidly in French.

'Are you sure you have the right station?' asks K. O'R. To him this is one of the most important events of the day. He takes his navigational duties extremely seriously, and nothing, nothing at all, must be allowed to interfere with them. Meals, sail changing, steering a course and other such trifles count for nothing.

'Yes,' I reply. 'You get the watch and stand-by. Big Ben will strike in a few minutes.'

Whilst I am pulling a blue jersey over my head comes the thunder and crash of the great bells. The set is tuned in far too loud but it amuses me to let it be so. Then comes the three tremendous reverberating clangs (we are two hours slow on GMT and plus one hour for BST makes the three-hour difference in time). Faintly, too, can be heard the time pips: presumably I have two stations overlapping.

'Three point two minutes slow,' says K. O'R in a voice of gloom. He would, I know, have used the same tone of voice no matter how slow or fast the watch had been. He distrusts that watch although it is, in fact, keeping very good time. I refrain from making any comment. Instead I enquire brightly as to wind and weather, course and speed. Having taken a sidelong glance at the log book to make sure it has been written up, and having noted that the barometer has risen very slightly, I climb up into the cockpit.

The night is as warm and soft as black velvet. Sea and sky are merged into one great blackness. But soon my eyes become used to the darkness and I can see the horizon showing faintly against the jet black of the sea. There is a pleasant little wind from somewhere and I turn to face it, testing it for strength and direction first on one cheek and then on the other. NNE I decide, about force 2. Holding on to the gallows I peer over the transom stern. A streaming wake of phosphorescence sparkles like quicksilver. I gaze at it entranced. Then I carefully search the horizon for steamers' lights before stepping down into the cockpit. There is no dew and the teak grating feels warm and dry under my bare feet. But I have not many clothes on, so I will go below again and find myself some occupation to kill the time until I can say 'Four o'clock, four o'clock,' and return to the comfort of my bunk. Firstly, however, I will find two biscuits, spread them thickly with peanut butter, and eat them.

First Days on Land

Alain Gerbault
The Fight of the Firecrest
first published 1926
(Mariners Library 1955)

Alain Gerbault's transatlantic voyage in 1923, in a former racing yacht designed by Dixon Kemp, Firecrest, *is legendary. The following extract is typical of the gear problems he encountered throughout the trip:*

Whenever the wind rose to a moderate gale something would give way. While I was mending the balloon forestaysail, the port steel wire runner, which steadies the masthead when on the starboard tack, parted and I had to stop sail-mending to put good rope in place of steel wire. While I was at work on the new runner, the jib sheet pennants broke. Next day the bobstay parted again and I had to splice it. If I took in the mainsail to repair it I had to hoist the trysail in its place. Then, no sooner had I finished repairing the mainsail than the trysail would give way, and I had to be busy again with palm and needle.

I am not given to superstition, but Friday, July 13th, was exceptionally bad. The *Firecrest* rolled horribly, the seas ran very high and things had been breaking aboard since dawn. Early that morning a big hole appeared in the forestaysail. I took it in and was letting the boat steer herself before the wind with the balloon foresail boomed out when the spinnaker boom broke, and fell overboard.

Walking out on the bowsprit to try to recover it, I put my feet on the cross-tree (or whiskers) which spreads the bowsprit shrouds. It broke under me and I fell into the water, but I caught hold of the bobstay and managed to crawl back on board ship. All this time the boat was steering herself, and doing more than three knots. Had I missed the forestay I should have stayed alone in mid-ocean. After that the narrow deck seemed particularly comfortable!

However on his arrival at New York after a voyage involving extraordinary privations, Gerbault found that his story caught the imagination of the public, with the most surprising results.

I had dropped anchor before an American fort, and at daybreak soldiers helped me to lay the *Firecrest* alongside a wharf. At once a crowd of curious camera-men and reporters came aboard. They were all surprised to learn that I had come from France. The Greek steamer had reported me, but everybody had believed it to be the joke of a French fisherman lost on the banks. Many actually thought that I was a bootlegger.

I had not spoken to a human being for three months, but was now obliged to answer the endless questions of the newspapermen during a whole day. I also had to face the camera-men and, though I had not slept for three days, was obliged to climb up the mast several times to please them.

The privacy of my floating home was soon and constantly invaded by a crowd of visitors. I had to obey the tyranny of far Western civilisation. And in this connection I well remember that it was painful to start the wearing of shoes again.

But I had lived too long in a world of dreams to be able to put up for long with the routine of daily life in a big city, and was constantly thinking of the happy days at sea. So strongly did these thoughts recur that, soon after landing, I was dreaming of putting to sea again.

But I still have many charming souvenirs of my stay in New York, nor will words tell what I owe to a certain captain and his wife, my first visitors aboard, who made my stay at Fort Totten a joy and a delight.

The American yachtsmen treated me like a brother. Bill Nutting, the hero of a famous passage across the Atlantic, became one of my best friends. Nor shall I ever forget a lecture I gave at West Point, when two cadets came and told me of their intention to leave the army and sail round the world in a small boat.

The American newspapers had been describing the cruise, but it was humorous, and even painful, to read the extraordinary accounts about it. Every newspaper seemed to want to print something new and startling, whether accurate or not, and in one I was surprised to read that I had on one occasion been unconscious for two days.

I was unknown when I landed, but on the morrow I found I had achieved a sort of bubble fame. Letters and telegrams began to arrive from everywhere, and were so numerous that an army of stenographers would have been necessary to deal with them.

Numerous, too, were the letters of friends, sincere friends, who were really pleased with the success of the cruise. But more numerous were the letters of strangers desirous to join me on my next cruise.

They were all sorts, eccentrics who wanted to become famous, and boys and men sincerely attracted by the lure of adventure.

Very uncommon was the letter of the Californian girl, who wrote:

'I am apt to do everything which is uncommon. When I read about your daring exploit I felt that I ought to do something myself. You know that a man is supposed to have more courage than a woman. I am merely a woman, being only twenty years old, and I have just completed a hike from Los Angeles to Milwaukee, having walked alone two thousand miles. The darker the night the better I like to be alone. I enjoy hearing coyotes howling when I am all alone . . . I don't know what it is to be afraid. One day I hope to go to Africa. I don't know what I shall do there, but I'll do what other people are afraid to do . . .'

She concluded by saying that the job of cabin-boy would fulfil her dearest dreams.

Another American girl had certainly a curious idea of life aboard for, having demonstrated that I could not again start alone, she claimed that she was very adaptable and that any job aboard from cabin-boy to 'social secretary' would suit her.

Very keen seemed to be the young girl who wrote:

'I have wasted the first twenty-five years of my life regretting I have been born a girl and not a boy. Now I am going to act just as if I was a boy. To be a sailor, and sail out to the South Sea Islands, has always been my dream. Of course I know that sailing alone with you will not seem very *comme il faut*, but why should we pay any attention to the conventions if we do what we think is right? If you have no sense of humour you will think I am mad, if you have some you will perhaps think the same.'

Charming was the letter of a young French girl, who wrote to me from a restaurant, and wanted to sail with me to cook my meals and sew my sails.

From Australia I received a letter written by an old French sailor, which contained a single five-thousand-word sentence filling sixteen pages, with numerous additions between the lines. I was never able to read the letter entirely. The poor lunatic wrote that he had been persecuted by the French consul, and that it was a great pity that the Channel Islands, which were so near the French coast, did not belong to the French. He suggested that I write to the King of England about it and that, after my exploit, he would be obliged to grant my demand. He added that he was writing at the same time to Sir Thomas Lipton to place before him one of his inventions for increasing the course and velocity of yachts, which would permit them to get back the American Cup to Great Britain.

Another inventor proposed to use in place of sails a windmill-like propeller that he had designed.

Curious, too, is a letter from Geneva.

'I am no more a young man, but I am still very strong. I am forty-eight years old, mineralogist, know all Nature's laws, and I would like to explore unknown countries. As I saw in the newspapers that you are going to visit some virgin islands, I am your man.'

The letter is signed—'A GOOD SWISS.

All these letters, however, were not letters from volunteers. Many children sent their congratulations, and these letters are very touching. They are, too, those one keeps and which give one the feeling that something useful has been done to raise the ideals of youth.

An eight-year-old child advised me not to sail towards the Pacific Ocean, which he knew to be dangerous. He seemed terribly anxious about me.

Another young American schoolboy wrote that he thought of me when seeing an aeroplane pass above his window. Also, 'I am going to work very hard to make a lot of money, buy a boat like yours, and wander round the world; but I must leave you and finish learning my lessons.'

A professor in transcendental sciences wanted to predict everything that was going to happen during my next cruise, but I could not accept his offer, for it would eliminate all the unforeseen – adventure's greatest attraction.

All these curious letters are but a few among the many. But most of those I received were quite serious, and from people really attracted by adventure; people willing to give up their jobs to run risks; letters from people belonging to different classes of society; letters from sailormen, mechanics, students and wealthy people. They seemingly wanted to give up everything, and to ask nothing in return. These letters were the hardest of all to answer.

A French officer in command of a destroyer wanted to give up the navy to serve under me. I naturally could not accept the suggestion, but felt very proud of the honour.

A commander in the Russian Navy wanted to ship as one of the crew.

Very brief and business-like was the following letter:

'I am an old sea-dog, born on the northern coast of Norway, fifty years old, active as a young boy. Can do two things well. Sail a boat and cook. Can you use me?'

A volunteer I could have done very well without was one who thought he was qualified because he was very unhappy and tired of life. In fact, he wanted to join me on a dangerous cruise, hoping to lose his life.

The twenty-year-old mechanic had a high opinion of himself who wrote:

'I'm afraid of nothing, and I have exceptional nerves. You can dispose of my life as you choose. Consider my proposition. It is worth it.'

There was also the seventeen-year-old ex-schoolboy who gave of himself a long and complete description.

'For many years I have been attracted by adventure. When I was still young I was dreaming of travels and wrecks. I gave up my studies, for I did not like the idea of working in a town. I am studying English and mathematics while I am waiting for an occasion to satisfy my savage tastes. I adore the sea, the pampas adventure and the unforeseen. Unluckily I can't give you a fortune for your expedition, but I will give you my instruction, my willingness and my friendship.'

I have many times tried to figure out the mentality of the young man who wrote:

'I have for you the greatest admiration. The reason is very simple – your character is exactly mine.'

There was also a wonderful polyglot sailor-waiter in a Duval restaurant, who knew navigation, could repair sails and was prepared to speak fluently French, English, German, Italian, Spanish, Norwegian, Danish, Swedish and American.

Perhaps the plumber would have been a good companion, who had no knowledge of maritime matters, but was fond of running, and a keen cyclist. He offered me all he owned, two thousand francs, and good health.

Another volunteer seemed to possess a rare gift for scribbling which would help me to write my books. I have, too, often thought of the big things I could have done together with an old sea-dog who had been at sea for fifteen years, did not want any wages and would follow me to death.

Another seaman, a volunteer of thirty, who had crossed the line twelve times aboard three-masted square-riggers – he gave descriptions of the dangers of the Pacific and of a typhoon in the Tonga Islands – wanted to follow me, and would not hold me responsible whatever happened.

I liked very much the letter of an American boy who sent me his photo at the wheel of a Gloucester schooner, and wrote:

'I should like to go with you. I have been at sea aboard steamers, and I worked aboard a schooner for two months. Of course, I have papers to prove it. I am eighteen years old, five foot ten inches in height, and my weight is one hundred and fifty pounds. I am young, willing, and I am not afraid of work. If you need money I think I shall be able to raise some, but of course a boy of my age cannot be expected to be very rich yet.'

Of what wonderful value in new surroundings would have been the quartermaster who had been at sea since he was ten years old, and had been four times round the Horn. He wrote:

'Take me with you. I am afraid of nothing. I shall always obey you. Back home we should be able to teach the French to love the sea. If you want it, I am yours body and soul for this great task.'

An English boy, a salesman in a great motor-car firm, wanted to give up his job to follow me. He would have been, I think, a splendid companion.

'Although I have a good position I am wasting my life when the sea and adventure are calling me louder and louder every day. During the war I served in the navy aboard boats hardly bigger than yours, cruising on the northern coast of Scotland. I am longing for adventure, and to see the very islands to which you are sailing. Can you take me with you? I am prepared to face any hardship for the love of the enterprise. If I had money I would give you everything I own.'

I was especially sorry to have to disappoint the thirteen-year-old Irish volunteer, who wrote:

'You will find me very useful when things have to be done in a hurry. I should prefer no wages.'

The letter is signed – 'Respectively yours.'

When I re-read all these letters – letters which I shall always keep with me – I cannot help thinking of the great drawing power the sea has when so many strong and energetic men are ready to throw up everything for adventure upon it.

But if I actually took anybody with me it would be as a companion, for I should prefer to do all the work myself.

It was really sad to have to disappoint so many who evidently had a real fondness for the sea, and perhaps this letter from a French sailor was the most difficult to reply to in the negative. He wrote:

'I am longing for the sea. I should like to wander again on the immensity of the ocean. I should like to live again a sailor's life, with its sufferings and its pains. I pray you to take me with you. I shall face without complaining the worst storms. I should like to be with you, sharing your life and those days without a morrow. I ask nothing. I shall bring nothing with me. I don't want to bring back anything. I implore you to take me with you.'

It was, in any case, the most pathetic letter I received, and has been placed between my favourite books – John Masefield's ballads and Bill Adams' short stories. It was a letter written by a real sailor, and one able to tell of his great passion for the sea.

The spirit of adventure to-day is anything but dead if one may judge by these few extracts.

A Flare for Invention

J D Sleightholme
Old Harry's Bunkside Book
first published 1978

The author writes:

Since 1959, when Old Harry first appeared on the scene, I seem to have written around one hundred and fifty short pieces about him. I was on the staff of Yachts and Yachting *then and Old Harry was an accidental invention, based subconsciously upon just about every obdurate, bloody minded traditionalist of inventive turn that I had ever chanced to meet. The Old Harry drawing, invented at the same time, has by sour coincidence come home to roost nearly twenty years later; I am assured by those around me that I have grown to look exactly like him.*

Prior to being taken over by my creation I have been inclined to sneer in fine contempt at writers who talked about giving 'life' to their characters. It smacked of a mimsy conceit, dirndl skirts and a mucky kitchen. The fact of the matter is that it is readers who force life into the monster, pull the switch and let loose the lightning and the author does damn-all. The Old Harry image now hangs around my neck with every mooring buoy I miss and with every sewer outfall pipe I hit. Sailing and yacht clubs everywhere seem to claim at least one Old Harry among their membership – a claim inspired more by resignation than pride.

A yachtsman and his distress signals is like the seasoned and cautious traveller who won't stir without a toilet roll in his luggage. Without them neither feels safe, both hope never to need them and both know that there is no acceptable substitute for either in case of emergency.

There is the owner who buys the cheapest possible pack (of flares), or is motivated more by an artistic appreciation of colour ('he gets it from his mother's side you know') than by stern judgement. The yachtsman regards his flares with begrudgement, like a commuter with his costly season ticket – having paid more than he can afford for something he didn't want in the first place.

In any case all too many yachtsmen start popping off long before their own resourcefulness is exhausted, and for reasons that vary from an inability to receive Radio One to a desire for company. Genuine cases tend to delay too long or to divine, with an uncanny accuracy, the moment when lifeboatmen ashore are about to put on their carpet slippers. Regarding the RNLI as an adjunct to the National Health Service, they summon the life-

Fig. 44

boat with the same easy confidence applied to their local GP ('My mother's got this nasty looking knee, doctor'). Both invitations are attended with promptness unrelieved by deep interest or pleasure.

'I see sir,' says the cox of the ILB, wringing water out of his beard, 'so you really must be back in Town by 10.30. Oh naturally you sent up six parachute flares and a Day Smoke sir. You could also have exhibited Flames In The Vessel sir, . . . an internationally accepted distress signal of great efficacy sir.' The owner, unaware of this method, shows immediate interest. The Coxswain smiles evilly. 'Now here's the way to go about it sir . . . ,' he explains.

Old Harry would never admit to being in need of RNLI assistance, although on the occasion of being reported to be perilously aground on a pinnacle he received the arrival of the life-boat with good grace. 'What's this then? Flag Day?' he asked humorously. 'Since you lot just happen to be passing by I might accept a bit of a pluck off.' The crew in their boat, like an Easter nest of stubbly yellow chicks, wrapped him in a blanket and dragged him struggling into their cuddy where they plied him with very hot water bottles and practised the Schafer Method on him with unnecessary energy and grim satisfaction.

Old Harry's flares were time-expired when Grace Darling was still being potted. Great dun-coloured cylinders with conical wooden warheads and a 6 ft pole, they are guaranteed to be armour piercing on the way down, in the unlikely event that they should ever go up. In fact, as he managed to demonstrate while using a blowlamp to discourage some fungus in his futtocks, they went sideways.

At the time, he was laid alongside the Town Quay, and like some awesome godly vengeance from Norse mythology, it went screaming up the High Street. A lady traffic warden, bending to read a meter, straightened up with a twang of elastic and dropped a couple of digits, while a solicitor's clerk, up to no good in firm's time, slammed the desk drawer and flattened his Dinky Toys. A cop on point duty was left pirouetting heavily and bounding around like Dr Scholl testing out a new corn plaster, but it was a gossiping matron, shaped like a middle ground buoy and taking leave of her friend, who rounded the show off. 'My goodness, I'm all behind today!' she said with unwitting candour. 'Bye, I'm going to fly now!'

Old Harry is reported to the Coastguard with the regularity of suburban nature lovers hailing the first cuckoo. Old ladies in seafront bed-sitters, maintaining their 24-hour vigil over the shameful goings-on in the wildly rocking beach huts, also follow his erratic maritime manoeuvres with puzzled attentiveness. 'No madam,' says a sighing policeman to his telephone, 'what you can see is probably a trick of the light or a large telescope at a low angle.' 'No madam,' says a weary Coastguard, 'what you can see is probably a yachtsman rucking his nock.' 'Yes madam,' says a yawning RNLI Secretary at 4 a.m., elbow on pillow, 'we're always delighted to be told when you think you've seen something funny off the end of the pier. Perhaps you'll give me more details about this side-splitting occurrence.'

Ever a scientist at heart and with an eye to improvement, Old Harry once set about manufacturing rockets capable of greater duration and altitude. Using an ancient Chinese formula, handed down (with alacrity) until it reached Barking Municipal Free Library, he compounded sulphur, burnt straw and saltpetre with a variety of unguents and inflammable nostrums, packing all into a jumbo size Squeezy bottle and attaching thereto a stout curtain pole. Realising the need to try out his prototype far from the sea, he got out his bike and headed for open country and haunts of coot and tern – both, at that time, blissfully unaware of what was coming their way.

An ardent bicyclist in his youth, his plunging knickerbockered legs had shied more horses than Stephenson's Rocket. His career in the Barking Creek Wheelers Club came to an abrupt end when he caught his wheels in the tramlines. The open doors of the Depot received his hurtling form like Valhalla opening to Eric the Red, but it was the buttocks of a hulking inspector, bowed low as he sank his grizzled muzzle into a pint of tea, that ended both his careering and his career.

Strapping the huge pyrotechnic to the crossbar of his sturdy machine, he headed for the countryside, pedalling firmly and at a pace just adequate to preserve equilibrium. Mentally congratulating the Authorities on their wisdom is providing a white line along which he could navigate and acknowledging the friendly cries of passing motorists, he made good time up the motorway. It was both unfortunate and coincidental that the red hot dottle from his pipe should have ignited his blue touch paper. There was a roar and a great gout of flame from beneath his tool bag. Within seconds his speed attained and exceeded the prohibited 70-mile limit.

With admirable presence of mind he raised his feet to the handlebars in the stylish mode of his youth and began overtaking vehicles at a rate that left them swerving wildly in his wake. A nun in a Morris 1000, forsaking her wheel and fumbling for her beads, made a surprise and unauthorised entry at the front door of a Little Chef; a Dutch driver of a juggernaut was left juggling with his Bols. The police car that took up pursuit stood no chance at all. Losing his way in the smoke cloud, its driver took a slip road in error and arrested a bicycling midwife.

With one final resounding explosion and an eruption of stars, Prince of Wales Feathers, cinders, spanners and smouldering melton trouser seat, the display came to an end and Old Harry, decelerating, slid to a halt under the baleful eye of a motorbike cop, with rockinghorse teeth and an open notebook. 'I should never have eaten them sprouts,' commented Old Harry.

Collision
Marine photographers frequently use telephoto lenses to combat the problem of
taking pictures at moderate or long range which still show detail. This causes
distances to look foreshortened in the pictures, and so shots of two yachts
crossing tacks often suggest that a collision is about to take place. For these
reasons, picture 4a does not look too unusual, until you notice that the pulpit of
the boat on the left is just kissing the genoa of the boat on starboard tack, and
the bow wave suggests an extremely violent collision is in prospect. The two
yachts met at the cruiser class start for the Britannia Cup during Cowes Week
1973. Jan Pott, *a German Class 1 yacht, was the boat on the left, trying for a*
port tack start, and Griffin III, *The RORC club boat, was on starboard. As*
4b and 4c show, the yachts collided at quite an oblique angle, and Jan Pott's
long, sharp bow swept along the leeward side of Griffin. *The force of the*
impact did little to Jan Pott, *but* Griffin's *topsides were stove in and her*
chainplates shifted in the hull. Griffin's *mast broke neatly in two, and the*
repair bill was considerable. Exit one chastened helmsman (4d). The photographer,
who took the first picture with split-second timing, was Jonathan Eastland.

4a

4b

4c

4d